COPING
WITH
CA$H

COPING
WITH
CA$H

Peter Corey

Illustrated by
Mike Phillips

Scholastic Canada Ltd.
Toronto New York London Auckland Sydney
Mexico City New Delhi Hong Kong Buenos Aires

Scholastic Canada Ltd.

175 Hillmount Road, Markham, Ontario L6C 1Z7, Canada

Scholastic Inc.

555 Broadway, New York, NY 10012, USA

Scholastic Australia Pty Limited

PO Box 579, Gosford, NSW 2250, Australia

Scholastic New Zealand Limited

Private Bag 94407, Greenmount, Auckland, New Zealand

Scholastic Ltd.

Villiers House, Clarendon Avenue, Leamington Spa,
Warwickshire CV32 5PR, UK

National Library of Canada Cataloguing in Publication

Corey, Peter

Coping with cash / Peter Corey ; illustrated by Mike Phillips.

ISBN 0-439-98821-7

1. Money—Juvenile humor. I. Phillips, Mike II. Title.

PN6231.M66C67 2003   j332.4'02'07   C2002-904350-6

First published in the UK by Scholastic Ltd., 2000

6 5 4 3 2 1   Printed in Canada   03 04 05 06 07

Contents

Dedication

This book is dedicated to Peter Martin, the best accountant an author could possibly have. Without him, I wouldn't have any cash to write about!

DO YOU NEED THIS BOOK ?

Hello! It's your favourite author here! Oh. Sorry. That's sort of a presumption, isn't it? After all, you may never have read anything by me.

Who am I, anyway? Check the front cover. I'll wait.

Dum, dum, dee-dum dee-dum.

You back? Good.

No. I'm not Mike Phillips. Try again.

Dee dee-diddly dee dee dee.

I'd whistle, but I don't know how to write it.

Back again? Okay. Do you know who I am now?

I'm Peter Corey. Got it? Good.

And what I want to know is . . .

Do you need this book?

Well, if you've never read any of my books you probably need to know that if you don't like laughing, then this book is not for you.[1]

Also, if you're not interested in finding out loads of useful stuff[2] then this book is probably not for you either.

Likewise, if you've got no cash, then this book is definitely not for you, because you can't afford it.[3] But that's what this book is about — CASH. Getting it, losing it, holding on to it, spending it; even sniffing it and building totally pointless hamster cages out of it, probably. Because this book covers everything you can possibly do with money, and a few things that you can't. It tells you how money started, and some truly amazing facts about it — such as . . .

1: If you HAVE read any of my books, you probably need to know that as well!
2: OK — useless.
3: Unless you're borrowing it from a library, in which case it's free as long as you take it back on time.

WAIT A SECOND! You haven't paid for it yet! So I'll leave you to take care of that and look forward to meeting you again at the start of chapter one (next page). If you don't take care of it (i.e. don't get to own the book because you can't afford to buy it), then all I can say is that it's been nice meeting you, anyway. By the way — what did you say your name was? Peter Corey? Oh, no — that's me! *Doh!*

WHAT IS MONEY?

Welcome, new book owner. You're now a few dollars worse off. However, you are about to discover all there is to know about cash: how to spend it and how to hang on to it.[1] Incidentally, if you haven't bought this book but are still reading it, then just make sure that you don't drool or sneeze on it — somebody else might want to buy it, you know.

Anyway, if you now own this book you probably dipped your hand in your pocket and pulled out some money. Or you may have whined on and on and on until your parent dipped in and pulled out a bulging wallet. Or an old sock with a few coins tied in the corner, because people keep their money in all sorts of strange places: under floorboards, under mattresses, on top of wardrobes — even in *banks*! Weird!

1: Don't buy goofy books for a start! Only joking!

You see, money makes people behave in very strange ways and do very peculiar things. But what exactly *is it*?

Turning to the *Oxford Pocket Dictionary*, which is actually almost as large as Peter Mansbridge's bald spot, we find out the following:

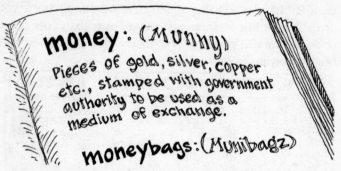

money: (Munny)
Pieces of gold, silver, copper etc., stamped with government authority to be used as a medium of exchange.

moneybags: (Munibagz)

Which presumably means to buy stuff. I love the way they say "gold, silver, copper etc." It just shows you how old my copy of the pocket Oxford is. These days, money is made out of anything that can be recycled without falling apart. Anything other than gold, silver, copper etc., anyway.

The *Big Book of Contemporary Slang* tells us that money can also be called Loot, Bread, Cash, Gelt, Folding Stuff, Loose Change, Moolah and any number of other things. None of which helps you get it.

Shakespeare tells us that "a fool and his money are soon parted." Not only a fool, actually; a quite sensible person, with no intention of spending anything, and *his* money are soon parted, especially if the person doing the parting is a time-share salesperson, or someone carrying a very large gun.[1]

The Bible, on the other hand, tells us that "money answereth all things"; that is, except *you* when you're looking for it. You know the score — you're late for the

1: Or both.

school bus, your only loonie has gone walking and you're standing in the middle of the living room going: "Loonie! Oh, loonie! Where are you? Come to me now, PLEEEAAASE!!!" And does it? Does it, diddly! It hides, keeping quiet as only a loonie can, until you positively have to run for the bus. And what happens when you come home? That very same loonie is sitting on the sofa, bold as brass,[1] almost smiling at you, as if to say: "I've been here all the time. In fact, I've spent the morning watching Regis and Kelly. They're worth their weight in gold."

"Worth their weight in gold": just one of the many expressions that some people use which relate to money — well, gold anyway. It basically means that somebody is very good at something, and well worth having around. So in Regis and Kelly's[2] case, it would be the wrong expression to use. "Not worth a plugged nickel" might be a better one! But in fact there are lots of expressions and sayings relating to money, such as . . .

"Money talks": although we've just found out that it doesn't.

1: Well — bold as reconstituted elephant droppings, which is probably what they make money out of these days.
2: For anyone from the planet Fibron, or somewhere other than North America, Regis and Kelly are TV personalities, apparently.

"Money has no smell": which means that, however money is obtained, there's no stigma attached to the actual money itself. People also refer to "dirty money," meaning money obtained in a dishonest or dishonourable way, which doesn't include money earned by washing your dad's car, although it probably should! The expression "Money has no smell" was first used by Vespasian, who was Emperor of Rome from AD 69–79. Apart from building the Coliseum and introducing a more comprehensive education system (so it's *his* fault!), Vespasian also introduced a tax on public lavatories.

When his son Titus complained that the tax was unfair, Vespasian held up a coin that had been collected via the toilet tax and said: "Does it smell?" Titus admitted that it didn't. "That's funny," said Vespasian, "It should. I've just fished it out of the toilet bowl!"

"Money is the root of all evil": meaning that everything bad is caused by money. Certainly money causes trouble, but I can't believe that *every* bad thing is caused by money. I'll take my chances, anyway!

"Money makes money": meaning that if you've got money you've got more chance of making more. Well, in my experience, if you've got money, you've got more chance of spending it!

"Money doesn't grow on trees": meaning that money isn't just lying around the place, except of course at the Royal Canadian Mint. In fact some money *does* grow on trees, in that some money is made of paper and paper comes from wood pulp, which comes from trees. But that doesn't make it any easier to get hold of.

The fact that people make up sayings and proverbs about money shows how important it has always been. But it doesn't stop at proverbs. Have you ever heard anyone, maybe your granny, mention pin money? She's probably mentioned it in between telling you how important string is. No? Doesn't ring any bells? I'm not surprised. After all, it's not always easy to figure out what she's talking about. But if you have heard her talk about pin money, you might even have wondered what it meant.

Well, she's not just rambling; it actually means something. These days it usually refers to a small amount of money not really worth thinking about, like a crummy wage (as in "I just got a Saturday job at the local branch of Burger Barons — I'm working for pin money"). But in the days when many women looked after the house and only men went out to work, it referred to money that a husband gave his wife for her to spend on herself (again, not usually very much). So what exactly *is* pin money? Simple — money for pins!

Pins were invented in France in 1543. They were considered a real luxury and not suitable for common people. Therefore, they were only on sale for two days of each year, some time in January. Husbands would give their wives money to buy these pins at the start of the year. Fascinating! Any husband who tried that now would get his head bitten off, particularly as many women have careers of their own and therefore their own money; which means that they can buy whatever they like — including pins.

Ah, money! We couldn't survive without it. Or could we? How do people who literally have no money survive? How did people manage before money was invented?

Let's start with that question and work our way through to the trickier ones. Yes! It's time to strap on a large canteen, slip into our desert boots and go trekking through the golden sands of time, trying to avoid poisonous sand snakes and ignoring the mirages. Ready? Let's go!

How money first started

It's not much fun living in a village that is largely made of mud. At least, that's what Wart Fatface thought, as he rubbed a damp clod of earth around his face. Wart had only recently moved to Floodybridge, a small village consisting mostly of a few houses, a church and . . . uh . . . a bridge that was regularly flooded. They really knew how to name things in those days.

Wart got his name from the large wart on the end of his nose. His surname came from the fact that he had a very fat face. His name was originally Wartnose V. Fatface,[1] but he had it changed by deed poll. Things could have been worse. He could have been the guy up the road with the terrible acne and hideous gas problem.[2]

Wart knew only too well that once you'd settled in a new village, the trick was to start a trade. After all, that was the only way to survive. Take Bigears Baker, for

1: The "V" stood for Very.
2: I'll let you figure his name out for yourself!

instance. He made the bread. Then there was Beerbelly Cooper who made the barrels for Nothumbs Brewer, who made the beer. He got his name from the fact that he had no thumbs; he lost them in an unfortunate exploding Christmas punch incident. There  was also Gorgeous Stitcher, who made exotic clothes for Snooty Bighouse, who owned the castle on the hill. In fact, everybody had a worthwhile occupation.

 Everybody except Wart, that is. The problem was that you had to have something to trade. Money didn't exist. If Beerbelly Cooper wanted a loaf, he would offer  Bigears Baker a barrel for it. A small barrel, obviously. But what happened if Beerbelly didn't have a small barrel, only large ones? Well,  they probably worked out a system whereby a barrel would be worth — say — twenty loaves, and Beerbelly would have to trust Bigears to make a note of how many loaves he owed him; which was a problem, because Bigears couldn't write. Even if he could, it wouldn't have helped, because Beerbelly couldn't read. Reading and writing were for rich folk like Snooty Bighouse. Oh, yes — you could really go places if you could read. Except the library, obviously, because libraries didn't exist then.

But how was somebody like Wart, with nothing to trade, going to survive in this sort of environment? Well, he could do little jobs for people, and receive goods in exchange. For instance, he could help Beerbelly make barrels, for which Beerbelly might give him some wood. Wart could then trade this wood with Bigears Baker for a loaf of bread.

But there was a problem with this system: suppose Bigears didn't want wood? Wart would have to trade his wood with somebody else (who did want wood), in order to get something that Bigears wanted, so that Wart could get his loaf of bread. This was called bartering, but as you can see it was pretty complicated. Something needed to be found that could replace the various goods that people wanted to trade, so that people could get the stuff they needed quickly and without a huge fuss — or before they starved to death!

The stone money age

Around 3,500 BC, people started using flint to barter, because flint was really useful for making arrow heads, axes and little flint novelties for the tourist trade.

I suppose the only problem with that was how much flint you had to "pay" to get what you wanted. Was your shard of flint big enough to buy a loaf of bread, or only a couple of sandwiches?

A few odd coppers

In Egypt, in about 2,500 BC (which is over four millennia ago), they started using copper rings as "money." Again, I suppose the value of the ring depended on its size and thickness, and this probably led to lots of arguments.

Copper was obviously something that they had lots of, just as other places had plenty of flint. At about the same time in Mesopotamia, they found that they had plenty of silver and barley lying around, and so they started using those as "money." And because they weighed the silver, they knew exactly how much it was worth. They made it into small lumps called shekels, which all weighed the same. This was a much better system, because it was easier to tell how much the silver was worth. I'm guessing they weighed the barley as well.

If you're wondering where Mesopotamia is, I'll tell you: it's in Iraq. In fact it *is* Iraq. They changed the name from Mesopotamia to Iraq, probably because nobody could spell Mesopotamia. Mind you, I sometimes have a bit of trouble spelling Irak — sorry, I mean Iraq.

That'll do ricely!

Shekels didn't catch on everywhere. The ancient Chinese used rice for money. That must have been a bit tricky. Imagine running around with your pockets full of rice. One quick game of touch football and you've lost half of it. Also, there's the problem of swelling. Anyone knows that if you get rice wet it swells. So imagine you're out on the town, pockets full of rice, determined to have a great time. Suddenly it starts to rain, your rice swells and you can't get it out of your pocket. Not very useful if you're trying to impress your date!

Realizing that rice money had its own problems, the Chinese introduced money in the shape of miniature gardening tools. I'm not quite sure what the exchange rate was, but maybe one spade was worth three hoes or something like that. Miniature gardening tools? You'd think those would be tough to get out of your pocket too!

Funny money

But gardening tools weren't the strangest things ever used for money. In Ghana they used pebbles made of quartz — this was before they started making watches out of it. The people of India used shells, Tibetans used metal discs, the Yap islanders used limestone discs and in Santa Cruz they used feathers. Imagine? You'd stick your hand in your wallet and tickle yourself to death!

There has also been money made of cocoa beans in Mexico, banana seeds in Uganda, lengths of telephone wire (!) in Tanzania, blocks of wood in Angola and eggs in Vietnam. Oh — and the people of Papua New Guinea used dogs' teeth. I wouldn't have wanted to be a dog around there, would you?

As late as the fourteenth century (700 years ago) people in the Sahara Desert were using salt as money. They kept it in large blocks and cut a chunk off, the size of which depended on the worth of the goods they were buying.

Raiding and trading

As civilizations grew, they started exploring the areas around them. They quickly discovered that there were other people living nearby. Explorers would return home and say: "There's this bunch of really strange people living over there. They look funny and talk funny, but they have some very nice stuff that we don't have and that just might be worth having." In those days, there were basically two ways to get your hands on somebody else's stuff: you could either take it by force, or trade it for something of your own. Sometimes it was just impossible to take things by force; the other civilization was bigger and tougher than you were. The only option was to trade. Merchants from one country would load their ships with local goods and take them off to trade with other nations. For example, the Romans took oil, wine and wool, and traded it for spices, grain and silk.

All of this was fine and dandy if the things you had to trade with were small enough to get on a ship. But what if all you had to trade with were cattle? You couldn't get many cows on the average ship in those days. A lot of them died on the journey, and you also couldn't be sure that the people at the other end would want them, any-way. A better system needed to be created. Unfortun-ately that wasn't going to happen for a very, very long time.

Loose change

The first coins (as far as we know) were made in Lydia — or Western Turkey to you and me. They were made by mixing gold and silver to create a sub-stance called electrum, then casting it into a rough pebble shape and stamping a picture on it: a lion, in fact (not a turkey!). King Croesus (560–546 BC) had coins made of pure gold, which he had lots of.[1]

The Lydian coins were made in about 700 BC, and pretty soon other countries were copying the idea and inventing their own coins, most of them made of gold or silver. But why use such precious metals? Why not use a lump of old iron or something?

The reason they used gold is because it looks nice, doesn't rust and it's also easy to hammer into shape and stamp with a picture. It's also pretty rare, so people couldn't start making their own coins and passing them off as the real thing — although I doubt that kept them from trying!

"Heads"

The first ruler to have his head on a coin was Alexander the Great — the ruler of Lydia. When Julius Caesar was

1: Hence the expression "as rich as Croesus."

murdered, the Romans brought out a special coin — a bit like the special commemorative coins we have these days. But coins were still only being used locally. They weren't being used to trade with other countries, who had their own coins.

Roman around with a pocket of loot

As the Roman Empire expanded — that is to say, as the Roman army swept across Europe, building roads, putting in plumbing and sticking their swords into any of the locals who complained — so the use of coins spread. The Romans had been using *rude* bronze, which didn't mean bits of bronze hammered into naughty shapes, but lumps of unworked bronze. Oh, and they also used salt. Roman soldiers were paid in salt.[1] You can easily imagine the problem this gave them. For a start, there really was nowhere in the soldier's uniform to store the salt; no pockets or anything.

At night they could put it into the belly button on the front of their breastplate, which obviously made it easy to keep people from stealing it; but it was not ideal when you were on the march. The Roman authorities, who were on the ball, replaced salt and bronze with coins

1: This is where the expression "not worth his salt" comes from.

toward the end of the first century AD, mainly in order to pay their huge army, who were frankly getting fed up with being paid in salt, twigs, banana seeds or anything else that happened to be currently serving as "money."

Of course, the soldiers couldn't actually spend the coins even when they got them. Imagine the scene: it's a lovely summer's Thursday evening in Gaulus (later to be known as France). Timurus and his pal Libatius have the evening off. They've had a tough day putting peasants to the sword, and all they want now is to find a bar, have a few drinks and then maybe go on later to a disco.

They're standing at the bar of Le Olliday Inne, a popular nightspot in those days. They're watching the cabaret, which seems to be some sort of local folk dancing. In fact, it's a couple of Gothic slaves leaping around barefoot on a large sheet of metal. There's a fire beneath the metal keeping it nice and warm, just in case they forget the dance steps.

The barman brings them a couple of glasses of the local wine — a wine so recently crushed that it's still got bits of toe jam floating in it. He is about to tell them how much it is when they slap a handful of small disks of metal on the counter and tell him to *keep the change*. This is an instruction that he doesn't understand for a number of reasons:

1. He's French and speaks absolutely no Latin — having never felt the need to learn, and having never been to school.
2. He doesn't even know what *money* is, let alone *change*.

So that's two reasons, in fact. Anyway . . .

This conversation might have continued for a very long time, if the Roman Empire hadn't collapsed and the soldiers gone back to Rome. But this was one of the big snags with money — it was all well and good if you wanted to spend it in your own country, but if you were off on a conquering tour or a cross-border shopping trip, you were out of luck. Of course, the coins were often made from gold and silver, which are valuable in their own right. But there wasn't that much of it, so coins were pretty rare. And you couldn't spend them abroad, which is why things like salt and grain continued to be used for trading.

Salting it all away

Of course, things like salt weren't used to show how wealthy a person was. You didn't, for instance, hear people say things like: "That Abu Ben Nevis is a wealthy guy — you should see the huge piles of salt he's got!"

Wealth was measured in things like precious metal (gold and silver) made into jewellery, and cattle. People *would* say: "That Abu Ben Nevis is a wealthy guy — he's got a hundred cows." Or maybe camels, if you were living in the Sahara Desert. Cows had also become an early form of currency. In fact, the word pecuniary, which means "to do with money," comes from *pecus*, which is a Latin term for cattle.

Middle Age spread

By about the fifth century AD, after the fall of Rome, many European states had been created; and they each had their own coins, which were very nice-looking but still no good if you wanted to travel. Sometimes individual cities would mint their own coins, and because the Church was very powerful in those days, even bishops would issue their own coins. It all got very confusing, until money changers came into existence. These were like an early form of bank. You could take your coins issued by Derek the Bishop of Chester, and exchange them for the much nicer ones issued by Arthur the Intrepid, or if you were really lucky, you might get your hands on some of those really unusual ones issued by Uthuck the Totally Stupid.

DEREK   ARTHUR   UTHUCK

You probably still wouldn't be able to spend them in your local Loblaws[1] though, because Loblaws was still hooked into the old barter system — this week's special offer was a chicken ("Keep it as a pet, then have it for a lunch!") which cost just three shards of flint and a feather.

1: This wasn't Loblaws as we know it, of course. It was a store run by Erthric Loblaw, the Body Snatcher, whose meat counter was always particularly busy during periods of plague.

One world — one coin

It was totally impossible to set up one type of coin for the whole of the then-known world, for a lot of very good reasons. The main one is that the various countries of the world were far too busy fighting each other; so the idea that they might sit down and work out a currency that suited everybody was a total pipe dream. In fact, in those days they couldn't even agree on one set of coins per country! This was mainly due to the fact that countries were divided into separate kingdoms with their own rulers. And each ruler wanted his or her head on a coin. And why not?

To be honest, ordinary people really didn't need money. They grew their own food and swapped (or bartered) any surplus for anything else they needed. Money was still very much a symbol of wealth and influence, neither of which your average peasant had.

The great leap forward

This system continued pretty well unchanged for several centuries. In fact, it remains unchanged in many parts of the world, where they still haven't seen any great need to use cash. All I can say is, very wise! But what about the so-called "civilized" world? Well, we have to make a huge jump forward in time to see any really big change in the way things were done. So, all together now . . .

Worth the paper it's written on, probably

It wasn't until as late as the sixteenth century (over 400 years ago) that paper money was introduced into Europe. In China, they'd actually been using it since AD 650. The reason for this was that metal money was heavy to carry around. Chinese coins originally had holes in them, because merchants used to string them together to avoid losing any. Of course, this also meant that if you were robbed, you'd lose it all in one shot!

It must have been very tempting for your average peasant, working away in a field, and seeing this sharp-dressed merchant coming along on his horse (camel, steer, goat, very large frog). It must have been even more tempting and tantalizing to hear all that money jangling around in his pocket, knowing that getting your hands on that cash would probably mean that you never had to work again,[2] and also knowing that there wasn't a police officer for miles around, because they hadn't been invented yet. As a result, merchants were often getting mugged. So what could they do about it? Someone — I don't know who — came up with the following idea: merchants would leave their coins with a goldsmith, who

2: Money being the universal symbol of wealth and influence.

would give them a receipt. The receipt would say something like:

Pimply Goldsmiths
promise to pay ..A..Merchant..
upon request .5.bags. of gold

Travelling light

This idea caught on and was developed so that the merchants could use it to make trips to other countries. Imagine this situation: a merchant from Paris (we'll call him Bill) wants to go to Venice, but he doesn't want to carry any money with him. Fortunately, he knows another Paris merchant (we'll call him Ben) who has an office in Venice. All Bill has to do is give his money to Ben in Paris, who will then give him a receipt. On Bill's arrival in Venice all he has to do is go to Ben's Venice office, show them the receipt and collect his money. And, as long as the merchants trusted each other, the system was foolproof. Unless somebody stole your receipt.

The bank

As this system developed, silversmiths and goldsmiths started getting together to form banks. The idea was that instead of issuing separate receipts, the bank would produce its own receipts, known as "banknotes," each worth a certain amount of gold.

Each bank issued its own banknotes, which must have become very confusing. Eventually this system settled down and central banks were established. The first bank in Europe was the Stockholm Bank, in Sweden, in 1661. Why Sweden? Well, I guess the Vikings (who came from Sweden) had made so much money robbing people that they thought they'd better put it safely in the bank, just in case somebody tried to rob *them*!

Each banknote issued by the Bank of Stockholm was worth a hundred *dalers*,[1] or silver coins.

(Of course, banknotes in Canada come from . . . uh, the Bank of Canada, which was founded in 1935.)

Incidentally, some countries' banknotes say something to the tune of "I promise to pay the bearer on demand the sum of . . . " and that sum depends on the note. What all this means is that if you go into the bank, hand over your banknote and demand whatever the note is worth, the bank promises to give you its value in precious metal. Except that it doesn't. The promise no longer applies.

1: Which is probably where dollars comes from.

All the banks will do now is change your banknote into other notes (or coins) worth the same value. They no longer hand over huge lumps of gold, even though they sometimes promise to do so on the note. And it's no good arguing with them. It's not even worth demanding to see the person who signed the banknote. Try going into the bank and saying: "Can I have a word with D.A. Dodge about getting my hands on twenty dollars worth of gold?" and see how quickly they show you the door. They just don't do it anymore. Banks are pretty good, but they don't have that much raw gold lying around.

Hey! I've just found a $10 bill signed by Elvis Presley . . . that'll be counterfeit.

The coins in your pocket

So now you know, roughly, how money started. Obviously, buying things is now far more sophisticated than simply handing over cash. For example, there are credit cards, debit cards and electronic banking. You can even pay for things over the phone. But for most of you, this is something that you don't really have to think about at the moment — you're probably far more concerned about the cash in your pocket, or lack of it.

To be honest, the easiest way to keep track of your money is to use cash. And if you're anything like me, then keeping track of your money isn't a problem. That's my money over there — those little round brown things; six cents altogether. But cash is what this book is about, so . . .

LET'S TALK CASH

Can you remember...

The first time you handled money? I'm not talking about that dime you shoved up your brother's nose, or even the dollar coin you swallowed.

WHY DID YOU JUST SWALLOW THAT LOONIE?

IT WAS "LUNCH MONEY"

I swallowed a dollar coin when I was little.[1] My mum took me to the doctor, and the doctor said that I'd have to wait and it would pass through me. So every morning, my mum, being very careful with money, put me on a potty and checked to see if the money had turned up yet, but there was no change.[2]

Probably the first time you handled money was at preschool, although it would have been plastic and smelled of spit-up. You probably thought: "This money is disgusting. I never want anything to do with it!" Little did you realize then that you would probably spend the rest of your life chasing after money and trying to hang on to it. But then, life is strange and cash is even stranger.

Can you remember...

The first time that you were in a store with your parents, and they handed you a five-dollar bill and said: "Give the money to the man, honey." You probably thought: "Do I look like my head zips up at the back? This is the first

1: Which was a clever trick, because they weren't around then.
2: No change! Money — no change! Sorry about that!

time I've ever had my hands on one of these things and I'm hanging on to it." You then promptly crumpled it up and poked it into your ear. But this would have been your parents' way of trying to teach you how to pay for something. Strangely enough, the older you get, the less eager they are for you to spend money, which doesn't seem right, somehow.

NOW THAT I'M OLD ENOUGH TO REALLY ENJOY WASTING MONEY, MY PARENTS WON'T LET ME NEAR IT!

Can you remember...

The first time you had some money of your own? You probably can't, because you were probably only a few months old. Sometimes when you're born, relatives give you money, which your parents then spend on really hideous clothes for you; the sort of stuff that you'd never be seen dead in if *you* had control of the purse strings. Some relatives give you cheques, which your parents forget to put in the bank for you; or they put them in their own bank account and forget all about them.

ABOUT THIS MONEY YOU'VE BEEN KEEPING SAFE FOR ME...

OOOOPS!

Of course, if you're *really* unlucky you get strange things made of silver that are no use to anybody: little trains, Humpty Dumptys and silver spoons with your name, date of birth and other intimate details engraved on them. Years later, you find these peculiar gifts gathering dust in a drawer.

"What is this thing?" you ask your mum.

"Oh, your Uncle David gave you that when you were born."

"That figures," you think to yourself. "He always was a weird one."

Can you remember...

The first time you were actually given money to handle? It was probably for something at school; cafeteria lunches, for example. Why anyone should have to pay for the privilege of getting food poisoning beats me. Or maybe it was for school photos or the school trip to the end of the street; or maybe the school was having a fundraiser to get the principal out of jail.

Whatever the reason, your parents will have pressed a sealed envelope into your hand, saying: "Be careful not to lose it." What a dumb thing to say! Obviously you're going to be careful *not* to lose it. What would be the point of being careful *to lose* it? And anyway, money can get lost very easily without any help from you. That's what money's like. One minute it's there, and the next it's gone. That's probably why your parents have sealed the envelope: they're worried about the money trying to escape.

Give me a break! They're worried about you stealing it, more like! Just imagine: for the first time in your life you've been trusted with an envelope stuffed with cash. You suddenly realize the truth of the maxim, "money means power" — or, in your case, independence. You think: "I'll run away!" Great idea! No more getting told off! No more having to go to bed when you're not tired! No more having to get up when you're fast asleep! No more having to have a bath when you hardly smell at all! Awesome!

CHING! CHING!

WE CAN RUN AWAY AND GET MARRIED NOW!

Little do you realize that the six dollars in the envelope won't get you to the other side of Mississauga (even if you *live* in Mississauga!) let alone to some paradise island where adults are illegal and the sea tastes of cola slush. Actually, it's unlikely to be six dollars; it's far more likely to be $5.79; something that involves your parents struggling to find change in the mad rush that is the

Monday morning pre-going-to-school panic. They will then find themselves four cents short and be totally convinced that the school "won't have any change." Actually, this is a myth devised by schools as a sure-fire money maker. Every time you offer anything other than the correct change (which is most times) the school says: "Sorry, no change!" and pockets the difference.

Anyway, having taken most of the furniture apart, ripped up the carpets and performed a tracheotomy on the dog (in case he's swallowed it), they eventually raid your piggy bank.

"Where did you get this $20 bill from?" Mom demands.

"What $20 bill?" you ask, as it disappears into her pocket.

The final outcome is that the required four cents is never found, your $20 bill is used to pay the school and the school keeps the change. Still, there is an up side: you get to feel the benefit of your twenty every time it's your turn to use the school pencil. OK, so that's only

once a term, and it's hardly the same as owning the latest CD by Hunks-R-Us, but it could be worse. No, it
couldn't!

Can you remember...

The first time somebody gave you money of your *very
own*? Money with no strings attached, or even bits
of elastic? Oh, Uncle Joe thinks that's so funny,
doesn't he? He turns up every Christmas with a
twonie in his hand; a twonie that he has carefully drilled a small hole into, and attached a
length of elastic to, which is even now running up the inside of his jacket sleeve and
secured in his armpit with an industrial-
strength safety pin. He offers the coin to
you, saying: "Don't spend it all at
once." As you reach forward to
take it, assuming that that is
what he wants you to do, the
coin shoots up his sleeve
with the speed of a super-
sonic jet, cracking three of
his ribs in the process. Judging from his laughter, he
obviously considers this a very small price to pay, considering the delight he gets from fooling you — *yet
again!* — into thinking that he was going to give you
some money. It's a stupid trick, but you fall for it, so convinced are you that money will solve all your problems.

Of course, you should have realized that the whole
thing was a con the minute he said: "Don't spend it all
at once."[1] It is impossible to spend a coin any other way.

1: You should have realized that it was a con the minute he started the whole
sorry business. The man's an adult, apparently. And you really should know
by now that adults cannot be trusted. Believe me, I know. I am an adult.

Consider this: you enter a store with a twonie. You want to buy the latest copy of *Birdwatching Monthly*. It's got this really interesting article about the pigeons on Parliament Hill.[1] And the magazine costs a dollar.[2] You hand over your twonie, thus *spending it all at once*. OK, so you're given change, but the twonie is gone forever, unless of course you sneak back later and rob their till, which frankly I've never really thought was a particularly good idea. The coins they give you in change are *different* coins; and they are also coins that you will eventually spend — *all at once*.

But to get back to your Uncle Joe. (Do we have to? I guess we should. After all, he's the only one in the family with any money, even if it is all attached to elastic bands up his sleeve.) If you really want to put him in his place — which quite honestly, should be a padded cell in the far reaches of Nunavut — then all you have to say is: "I see you've drilled a hole into this twonie, Uncle Joe. Did you realize that the penalty for defacing a Canadian coin is death, followed by a hefty fine?" That's bound to

1: OK, so I'm talking drivel. I'll get help, I promise; just as soon as I finish this book.
2: Ludicrously cheap by most magazine standards, but frighteningly overpriced for this particular publication, in my opinion. But then I'm not really into bird-watching. Or at least, I try not to be.

give him a crinkly mouth, and possibly a heart attack — which is only useful if he's made out a will in your favour.

Hold on a second!

I've just been re-reading this last part — checking for spelling mistakes, which frankly is a completely pointless exercise for me. My spelling is so bad that I wouldn't spot a mistake if it bit me in the legg. Ouch! No — the thing that caught my attention was not a yet-undiscovered way of spelling *mowth* — sorry, *mouth* — it was the phrase *millionaire lunatic*. One of the many things money allows you to be is crazy. If you've got buckets of cash you are allowed to be stark raving bonkers. Take the average rock star — they can go around looking like an exploded Salvation Army reject bin, and nobody minds. In fact, people *indulge* them. They can do no wrong. And all because they are *loaded*.

But you try being even a little eccentric, with those holes in your socks, and see where it gets you. Believe me, I've tried it — it doesn't work.

Can you remember...

The first time you were given money for something you had supposedly done? And I'm not talking about the reward you got when you turned in the neighbours for pirating cable.[1] I suppose the sort of thing that I'm thinking about is losing a tooth. That in itself is a contradiction; you don't actually lose it. It comes out. You know exactly where it is: it's embedded in the ear of that kid that everyone hates at preschool. What is odd is that the kid's mum isn't mad at you; in fact, she looks delighted. *Why is that?* you find yourself wondering. But then you stop wondering. After all, you're only three and at three, life holds even greater mysteries, such as why do you always start peeing just before you get to the toilet. Weird, isn't it? Anyway, you get your tooth back — after a bit of a fight, which the teachers seem to be encouraging — and Mum says: "Put it under your pillow." Listen, it's hard enough to sleep with those dismembered bits of Action Man and fifteen Beanie Babies under the pillow, without the added discomfort of a tooth, as well.

When I was little, I wanted to marry the Tooth Fairy. To be completely honest, I still do. After all, anyone who

1: Their daughter Mandy illegally copied a Backstreet Boys CD the other day, if you feel like snitching on them again. I think that's probably a crime on two fronts: illegal copying and having a Backstreet Boys CD in the house.

can afford to splash out a quarter (or a loonie) every time anyone *anywhere* loses a tooth, has got to be *loaded*. Sheesh! My mum had all her teeth out at once.[1] Think of how much that must have set the poor old Tooth Fairy back! But has anyone ever had a note from the Tooth Fairy, saying: "Can I settle with you at the end of the month? I'm a bit short right now." Of course they haven't! And who signs the Tooth Fairy's paycheques? Nobody! She has a private income. I'm telling you, she's loaded. Mind you, if you want to get your hands on her millions you'd have to let her take a large mallet to your teeth, but it would be a small price to pay.[2] I am assuming that the Tooth Fairy is female. There is a reasonable chance that she might be a man, in which case forget that part about me wanting to marry him. I'll settle for being really good buddies, and a cash handout.

But those first coins that people give you — even the ones from the Tooth Fairy — they're really special, aren't they? You hold them; you don't want to let them go. To you, they're not really money; they're something magical. Sound silly? Not really. Money is magical. It can disappear so fast that you don't even know it's gone.

1: OK, so it was a lucky punch. If she'd won, she would have been WBA bantamweight champion by now.
2: This is a very old expression. Frankly, these days there is no such thing as a small price to pay.

Can you remember...

The first time you were given allowance? Ah, allowance. Blood money, more like. Allowance is one of the ways that parents control their children. There are lots of others, but allowance is one of the least subtle ways. Does any of this look familiar?

Car washing and allowance should be totally separate issues. In fact, if you ask me, allowance shouldn't be related to household chores at all. (More of this later.)

But do you remember the time when you started getting allowance on a regular basis? I'm not talking about your parent grudgingly handing over a handful of small coins — most of them foreign — because you've demanded the much-promised regular allowance. I'm talking about a regular, never-missed weekly ritual involving your parents willingly placing an agreed sum

---

1: Actually, there's no such thing as "the car." That means my car. Parents like to try to pretend that their car is in some way the family vehicle — but try offering to drive, and see how far it gets you.

into your hand with no strings, no elastic and no very small print. Money that is yours to do with as you please.

Yes, you're right — that will probably *never* happen! But suppose it does. Oh, come on, we can dream, can't we? Just suppose that, for some reason, you do find yourself in possession of money that is yours to do with as you please. Maybe your parents have had an adult-personality bypass, or something. Anyway, whatever the reason, here you are with a fistful of dough that is yours and yours alone. You're on the town and *loaded*. Do you seriously think your parents are going to let you make such a big decision as how to spend your allowance *on your own*? Think again! There's this CD you want. Just as you're about to take it to the counter they appear at your elbow and say: "Hmm. Well, not a *bad* choice. But for a dollar less you can get this triple album of *Barry Manilow's Greatest Hits*. This cool new boy band/girl band will be forgotten by next week, but Barry will live on forever."

There's certainly evidence to back up the second part of this opinion.

"But I can't stand Barry Manilow," you whimper, already feeling that the battle might be lost. Moments later you are walking out of the store, CD dangling in a gossamer-thin plastic bag that not only is totally non-biodegradable but also emits toxic fumes. Through the plastic curtain that is the side of the bag, the entire world (plus all of your friends) can clearly read *Barry Manilow's Greatest Hits: A Millennium of Masterly Music*. The up side is that by saving yourself a dollar, you had just enough money to buy a set of earplugs, so it wasn't a totally wasted outing.

This has been just one short journey into the murky world of buying and selling. There will be many, many more. And it won't get any easier.

Money is power

You probably remember that I mentioned this earlier. If you don't, then it doesn't matter; you don't need to go back and check. More than any other thing, money can be used to manipulate people. We've already touched on the kind of moral blackmail that parents use to control you — threatening to withhold money for jobs not done, or offering cash inducements for jobs they want you to do. Nowhere will you feel this more strongly than on a family vacation.[1]

Wish you weren't here

Just imagine the situation: you've scrimped and saved for months. You've carefully salted away your allowance, despite the fact that there have been tons of things you've wanted to buy: computer games, CDs, videos, candy; the list is endless. Finally, the vacation looms and you've managed to save up enough money to ensure a totally cool time. It hasn't been easy. You've had to toss aside your principles in the pursuit of cash. You've done extra jobs around the house, you've made your bed

1: "Family vacation" is a strange expression. The only thing that ever really ruins a family vacation is having your family with you!

without being asked, you've been nice to your little brother, you've gone a whole week without arguing with your sister, you've cleaned out your rabbit's hutch, eaten all your peas, done your homework and even tidied your room! Heck — if you were on a proper salary, you'd be a multi-millionaire after doing all that.[1] And so, after the long car trip with all the obligatory vacation features, such as getting lost, community singing, throwing up, saying "are we there yet?" and the car blowing up, you finally reach your holiday destination — Power-Station-by-the-Sea.

OK, so it doesn't look too special, but you quickly deduce that there *are* things to do — not to mention that there's this cute girl/boy staying in the same hotel. Yes. This could turn into the vacation of a lifetime — just as long as the cash holds out. Because cash is the only way that you are going to be able to keep yourself independent of the rest of the family. With enough dough tucked

1: Yes, I appreciate that these jobs wouldn't normally generate cash, but this is the lead-up to vacation, and parents are known to be more generous around this time, aren't they? Aren't they? Oh — maybe that's where I'm going wrong!

into your back pocket you'll be able to go your own way, and nobody can stop you.

Oh, you think so, do you? Think again. Parents on vacation have ways of making sure that you stay totally dependent on them, and therefore within telling-off range. So how do they do it? Very easily, as it happens.

On the first day of the vacation you all climb into your matching plastic rain ponchos — yes! It's raining! Wouldn't you know it?

What makes it even more annoying is the fact that the last two weeks of school witnessed a heat wave. One kid actually spontaneously combusted because he was wearing an acrylic blazer. But the minute your vacation arrives, it's torrential downpours all around. You secretly hope that the school gets washed away in a flash flood — but it won't.

Anyway, there you are, looking like the Von Trapp Family Singers,[1] walking into the nearest souvenir shop to get gifts for those relatives who haven't had the good fortune to be on vacation (or misfortune, depending on how you look at it). Parents always insist that cards and gifts are bought on the first day. As a child I used to think that this was because the rest of the two weeks would be so stuffed with excitement that we wouldn't have time

1: From *The Sound of Music*. What do you mean you've never seen it? Where do you go every Christmas?

49

in our exhilarating schedule to squeeze in even two minutes of card buying.

"And don't forget to buy something nice for Granny," your mum warns, knowing that she'll never hear the end of it if you don't.

And so you buy postcards for everybody: relatives, neighbours, pets, neighbours' pets, relatives' pets, neighbours' relatives, relatives' neighbours, neighbours' relatives' pets, relatives' neighbours' pets, neighbours' pets' neighbours' relatives' pets. Friends. Friends' pets. Pets' friends . . . Oh, I think you get the idea! Anyway — back at the "hotel," a badly converted abattoir, you take stock of your new financial position. Broke. Penniless. So what are you going to do for money for the rest of the two weeks? Offer protection to your little brother in return for cash?[1] Forget it! He's even broker than you are, having blown all his cash on a large plastic turtle, which he just *had* to have. Once you return home — assuming that you all survive that long — the turtle will have pride of place in a hastily-put-together aquatic display involving Action Man exploring some bits of lettuce, dressed in a state-of-the-art diving suit made from a dishwashing-liquid bottle and toilet-paper rolls. By this time next

1: Protection from you, obviously — as in "pay up or I'll crush you!"

month, the turtle will have become a forgotten dust-gatherer who lives under the bed.

None of this solves your current financial situation, which is desperate. And that gorgeous girl/boy is waving at you right now! The fact is that you will spend the next two weeks walking six paces behind your parents, looking like an FBI agent stalking two escaped lunatics. Dad will be wearing a T-shirt with "I'm with this idiot" emblazoned across the front, and an arrow pointing at mum, who will be wearing a T-shirt which reads "Girl Having Fun!" — a statement that nobody will believe for a minute. Your entertainment will be entirely governed by what your parents want to do; which might be fine except they want to visit the Big Fish Centre which seems to consist of a small tank with a goldfish in it. The goldfish looks like it's been inflated with a bicycle pump to make it look bigger. Oh, and they also want to visit the local Co-op store, because it's a bit bigger than the one you've got at home. Unlike you, your parents will be having the time of their lives, *doing things as a family.*

As if you don't do that all year long. After all, you all live, eat, sleep and poop in the same house, don't you?

You even talk to each other occasionally, without being prompted.[1] What more do these people want?

By Tuesday, you're desperate. You've just spent the morning watching your little brother break the world record for number of jumps on a half-inflated bouncy castle. Unfortunately the man from the *Guinness Book of Records* wasn't there to witness it, but don't worry — dad's shot three rolls of film of it, so you should be able to make your own flip book of the momentous event. It's about now that you hear yourself whine:

Yes! Your parents hold the purse strings, so they are going to control everything, including your ice-cream consumption. But why are they doing it? Don't they want you to have a good time? Of course they do! But you don't have to spend money to have a good time, apparently. After all, think of all the lovely fresh air you're getting, wandering around like the Lost Tribe of Anorak. And it isn't costing you a penny! Mainly because you haven't got one.

Of course, the real truth behind this situation is far more sinister. Your parents won't be able to relax and enjoy the vacation unless they know exactly what you're

---

1: Mealtimes are the worst. Dad tells you to turn the radio off so that you can all have a decent conversation, and then the minute you try to start one he tells you off for talking while you're eating. You can't win — but then you probably already knew that!

up to, morning, noon and night (and all the times in between). The only way to achieve this is to make sure that you are totally dependent on them. And by making sure that you have no money of your own, they achieve exactly what they have set out to do.

And of course, it doesn't stop at vacations. There are lots of ways that parents use cash to control you. For instance:

Enjoy your trip

Yes! The good old school trip. Even if it's just a quick visit to the park with a bunch of other mixed-up toddlers, your parents have still had to cough up five dollars towards the gallons of bug repellent that Mrs. Eavesdrop the teacher will need, to keep herself from being eaten alive by small insects who don't have the intelligence to know that she's poisonous.

As you leave home that morning your mum issues a veiled threat; so veiled, in fact, that you probably don't even realize that it *is* a threat:

"Now, be on your best behaviour. This trip has cost me a lot of money."

Not that *you'll* cause any trouble. You're too sensible, for one thing.[1] For another thing, you have had the idea firmly planted in your head that one false move on your

---

1: Sorry — I didn't mean to call you sensible. After all, you wouldn't be reading this book if you were that sensible, would you?

part could take any further trips off the menu. OK, so it's only the park now — but once you get to high school you could be jetting off to really exotic places, like Niagara Falls. Or skiing in Switzerland.

Wow! That's a biggy. And don't your parents know it. They've been scrimping and saving for months so that you can go. Why are they so eager? Are they planning to move while you're away? No! They want you to enjoy yourself. Not too much, obviously, but they won't mind if you watch a bit of Swiss TV, or pay a cultural visit to a chocolate factory. But they start to work on you the minute the list of things you'll need comes through from school. And what a list! Why do you need seventeen sweaters? You're only going for a week! Surely Switzerland can't be that cold, can it?

Maybe this is the list for the entire school group, and for some reason your parents have been elected to provide it. If they had the slightest inkling about your parents' appalling fashion sense, they would never have bothered. Anyway, your parents take you off to the ski shop, where they start playing that game that all parents are really good at: appearing very generous by offering to buy you a skiing outfit, and then spoiling it totally by insisting on buying the only one in the shop that nobody would be caught dead in. And the further down the list you go, the worse everything gets.

"Will he/she really need sunblock? It *is* a little expensive," your mum says tentatively.

"Yes, unless you *want* them to come home looking like they've been involved in a nuclear accident."

A long pause for thought from your parents. They're surely not seriously considering this as a possibility, are they? And then comes the warning:

"Well, take care and make it last. You could use it for brushing your teeth, too. It does have a minty smell."

This continues with every item purchased, until you are standing amid a small mountain of neatly wrapped packages. You have been treated to a mountain of very expensive gear; you've also been treated to what your parent considers to be subtlety. But the message is very clear: my money went into this stuff, so screw up and you won't be able to move for the mountain of guilt that will crash down on your head. Actually, mess around on the ski slope and you probably won't be able to move for the plaster around your broken limbs, but that's another story.

Once more from the top

But if you think that money-based parental manipulation stops there, think again! Remember those piano lessons?[1] Great, weren't they? OK, so you weren't a natural pianist.

1: Or was it keyboard? I can't remember.

It took you three lessons to realize the piano lid was down. Why didn't your piano teacher point that out? Simple — she was charging by the hour, and the longer it took you to get the lid open the more she got paid. It soon became obvious, even to your parents, that as far as the piano was concerned, you were no Vanessa-Mae. (Which is just as well, because she plays the violin.) Because of this, your parents have opted to pay for one lesson at a time, and so the weekly ritual is as follows:

1. You tuck your piano music under your arm, ready to leave the house for your lesson.

I BET BEETHOVEN DIDN'T HAVE THIS TROUBLE!

2. You tuck the piano under the other. No! Only joking! You drag the piano on a small trolley behind you.
3. You stand in front of your parent in a sad pose that means: Can I have the money for my lesson, please?

Your parent then goes into a whole routine destined to make you feel:

A. Guilty that you're not a child genius.
B. Very, very humbled that your parents would go without important things like chocolate so that you can have a musical education.

Unfortunately, this doesn't work, because you never wanted piano lessons in the first place. Not that you're not interested in music; you are. But you've failed to find anyone who teaches paper and comb.

Still, the underlying message is clear: this is moral blackmail, plain and simple. In exactly the same way that you didn't dare step out of line on the school trip, for fear of letting your parents (and their money) down, so you bash away at the piano simply because your parents are paying for you to do it. Actually, bashing the piano could be where you're going wrong; you're supposed to hit those black-and-white things in some kind of order, not in batches of six.

By now I'm sure you can see how this parental-control-by-money thing works, and you can apply it to almost any situation you find yourself in where money is an issue:

OK, so that last one may not be such a good example, but I'm sure you get the idea. Actually, the pen one is a bit suspect too. And I don't think the excuse, "Sorry I haven't done my homework, Sir, but my mum refused to buy me a new pen," cuts a lot of ice with most teachers.

The curse of the coin

So is that what money's about? Salt, feathers and pieces of old metal that parents use to control you? Of course it isn't! It's far more complicated than that. So far I've just scratched the surface. To be honest, it would take a book the size of P.E.I. to cover all the mysteries of money.

I imagine that you're starting to feel that life would be a lot simpler if we didn't have to worry about money at all. Well done! You're absolutely right! Unfortunately, virtually everything we do involves money at one point or another, so we actually can't live without it. All we can do is learn to *cope*. And that's why I'm here! Have I ever let you down in the past? Of course not! Probably. So hold my hand and let me steer you through the complex world of cash. But be warned — it's going to be a bumpy ride!

THE A-Z OF COPING WITH CASH

What follows is a guide to some of the many facets of cash; the pitfalls and the problems, but also the joys and delights. In order to make it more manageable, I've arranged the various headings into cunningly simple, user-friendly alphabetical order. And to make things even simpler, I'm going to start with "A":

Accountant

What is it?

Look around your classroom. Go ahead — the teacher won't mind. Teachers like to see their pupils moving; it proves that they're still awake (and alive!). The kid over there who's especially good at math — can you see her? Well, one day she could quite easily be an accountant.

But what exactly is that? Basically, it's somebody who does accounts; although I guess you'd figured that much out for yourself. If you earn a lot of money — or if you're just useless with money (like I am!) — then you might need to hire an accountant to manage it for you. Don't worry, it's unlikely that you're going to need one to manage your allowance for you, unless you're very lucky (or your parents are even worse with money than I am). But as you get older and start earning, an accountant will keep records of everything you spend and everything you earn, sort out things like income tax for you, and generally help you handle your cash. Pop stars usually have armies of accountants working for them, and their job is to invest the pop star's money and hopefully make more money for him/her.

Again, this is not something you'll need, so why am I telling you? Well, remember when you took those home-baked cookies into school? Everybody said how tasty they were and asked you to bring in more. So what did you do? You made more and sold them in little bags for two dollars, didn't you? Great idea; very enterprising.

And you might still be doing it now, if that smart kid who knows everything hadn't spotted that they were dog biscuits coated in icing sugar. Huh! Some kids are just too bright for their own good, aren't they? It makes me sick, it really does! Anyway, if Smartypants hadn't rumbled your scam, your home-baked cookie empire would have grown and grown, the money would have been rolling in and you would have needed help to figure it all out. And that's where an accountant would have come in handy.

How to cope
There's not much to cope with. An accountant will cope for you. Finding a good one is the tricky part!

Allowance

What is it?
This is something that causes almost as much trouble in the average household as the argument about whose turn it is to forget to feed the animals. Logic tells you that

you should be getting as much allowance as your friends. After all, that's what they get; as much as *their* friends. All their friends except you, anyway.

Unfortunately, this kind of logic is lost on your average parent, who probably doesn't see why you *need* allowance, anyway. After all, you'll only spend it.

And this is where they miss the point. That's what allowance is for: spending. It isn't money that is attached to some specific job; at least it *shouldn't* be. And this is also another mistake that parents make. They firmly believe that allowance is something they give you in return for jobs that you do for them. No! Sorry, parents! That's just not right! Allowance is allowance; it's money for you to do with as you will. You're free to save it, spend it, give it away to a worthy cause; even give it back to your parents, if you really want to![1]

Of course, parents don't understand this. Some don't even see why *they* should be giving you allowance in the first place.

How to cope
The first thing you have to do is clearly establish that your parents understand the meaning of allowance. They need to realize that it's all part of growing up.

1: If you find yourself wanting to do this, lie down for a bit; the feeling will pass. If it doesn't, go and see a doctor — it's not normal!

Learning to handle money is an essential step along the rocky road to adulthood.

Some parents may try to get around this by letting you play with their money for twenty minutes on weekends, but you have to make them realize that this is not the same thing at all. The money has to be yours and yours alone. Yours alone — not *yours, a loan*; this has to be money they've given you to keep.

Having established that, and having got your hands on even a small amount of money, the big problem is going to be getting your parents to leave you to look after the money all on your own. This is part of letting go, and something that many parents find very hard. After all, they probably earned that money; they may even have had it for a long time. They've become attached to it; it's almost part of the family. Watching it go off to McDonald's without knowing whether they'll ever see it again can be deeply stressful. So you need to reassure them that you'll look after the money, see it safely across the road, etc., and never let it out of your sight. At least until you spend it.

It's a good idea if, the first few times you get allowance, you buy something you can take back to show your parents. If you're really brave you might even let them watch you spend it, although as I've said many times in this book, they'll only try to put you off. But if you can bear this, it is at least one way of letting your parents see that the money isn't gone, it's just turned into something else; transfigured, if you like.

After a while, if all goes according to plan, your parents will stop worrying about what time your allowance comes home; until eventually they won't care whether it comes home or not. You, of course, will always be a different matter. Whatever time you come home, they'll still want to know why you're so late. That is one battle you'll never win, I'm afraid!

Bank account

What is it?
This is the thing that the bank keeps people's money in. I did a bit of checking, which involved disguising myself as a very small child (if you've ever seen me, you'll realize just how tricky that was!) and going into the bank

with a fistful of Monopoly money. At first, they thought I was a very short bank robber and the teller pressed the panic button.

I must say that the police were very understanding, and once the tear gas had cleared we were able to have a good laugh about it, until the nurse told us that laughing wasn't allowed in intensive care. However, I'm now pretty well over the shock, and I did find out the following:[1]

As long as your parents go along with it, you can open a bank account in your own name at any age. If you want to be able to get your hands on your cash without them interfering (fat chance!) then your parents need to spell that out to the bank. Then, to take your money out of the account you just go into the bank, ask, and they'll give you your cash. But you must be able to prove who you are. It's no good saying: "Hand over my cash — the Teletubbies have the place surrounded," even if they have. Banks are not impressed by that sort of thing.

1: This information may vary from bank to bank. I went to the one that's got all my money (in a sock under the manager's bed).

Of course, keeping your money safely in the bank is not going to keep your parents from getting their hands on it. For all you know, the bank manager might even help them; after all, he or she is probably a parent too!

How to cope
Keep your money in a sock under the bed. But make sure that the sock is locked inside your piggy bank.[1] Better still, spend your money so you won't have to worry about losing it.

Banknotes

What are they?
These are also called bills or paper money.

Nice, aren't they? Especially when they're new. There's nothing better than opening a birthday card and seeing a crisp $20 bill flutter out. A word of warning here, however: if you think a birthday card is likely to contain a banknote, don't open it anywhere near the dog; dogs are so stupid, they'll mistake it for some new form of flying food and eat it. Do you have any idea

1: See also PIGGY BANK

how much a vet charges to cut your dog open to get a twenty back? Lots!

Anyway, having got your brand-new, crisp $20 bill, you start to fantasize about how to spend it. You make a list of all the things you want; by the time the list has covered two sides of one page in an exercise book, you realize that twenty dollars really isn't a lot of money. But it's all you've got, so you fold it carefully and place it safely in your pocket before setting off downtown for a shopping "spree." You've been extra-cautious; you've managed to avoid telling your mum or dad that you're going shopping, so there's no chance of them coming with you and offering to spend your money for you on something sensible. So what can possibly go wrong?

Well, I don't know whether you've noticed this, but banknotes have a nasty habit of disguising themselves as bits of scrap paper. It's basically a design fault that has never been cured. It doesn't matter how carefully or neatly you fold the bill and place it in your pocket, within minutes it will look like that old chocolate bar wrapper that you keep meaning to throw away. And you can bet all the money you like[1] that the moment you decide to throw out that wrapper is the moment that it isn't a

1: Although, of course, you can't bet any money *at all* if you've just mistakenly thrown it away.

wrapper at all, but your precious twenty dollars of birthday money.

How to cope

Thankfully, the Bank of Canada is trying to solve the problem for you. Banknotes are slowly being replaced by coins. By the time you read this there may well be a $5 coin, even a $10 one. The only worrying thing about this is the fact that each coin is bigger than the last.

My concern is that there will eventually be coins that are too big to carry in your pocket. Worse still — too big to hide from light-fingered parents!

But in the meantime, how are you going to cope with that $20 bill? Get a wallet or purse, preferably one with a huge combination padlock. I say combination lock because many parents are pretty swift at picking locks! Then place your neatly folded $20 bill into the wallet/purse and lock it up. That way, when you arrive at the store of your choice you can unlock your wallet and go: "Wait a second! How did that crunched-up old chocolate-bar wrapper get in there? And where's my $20 banknote?"

Birthday money

What is it?

This is the best kind of money, because it is all yours to do whatever you want with. That's the theory, anyway. In practice, it depends more on when you were born. I was born in the middle of August, for instance. Not only did this mean that I'd had a year less in nursery school than most of my friends, but it also meant that I was almost certainly going to fall victim to the massive back-to-school campaign that all the stores mount around the middle of August. Maybe it was my sad lack of education, or maybe I just wasn't as smart as other kids, but the minute the birthday money fell out of the envelope, my mum was saying "You need new school shoes" and I was agreeing with her.[1]

I say that the minute the money arrived the shoe conversation took place, but that's not exactly true. The minute the money fell out of the envelope, the thank-you letter conversation took place.[2]

Now, I can possibly be forgiven for believing that once we got to the shoe store, I would be allowed to pick my own new shoes. After all, it was my birthday, and my birthday money. Not at all. Or at least, not exactly. I *was* allowed to try on the latest fashions, but amazingly none of them fit.

"We just don't seem to have your size in the winkle-picker elastic-sided Chelsea boot,[3] sir," the clerk purred.

It wasn't until years later that I realized that my mum and the clerk were in cahoots. After all, they were both from the same planet — Planet Parent — and so they

1: See also UGLY SHOES
2: See also THANK-YOU LETTERS
3: Yes, I know they sound awful now, but I thought they were to die for. I did eventually get some and I've had foot trouble ever since, partly because my feet are now pointed.

were bound not to understand. Ironically, whenever I try the same trick on my own children I get the 15-year-old work-experience clerk who comes from the same planet as my kids — Planet Cool — and so I wind up spending a fortune on running shoes and getting hauled up in front of my son's principal to explain his "inappropriate footwear." Listen, buddy — all I did was pay for them!

How to cope

If you find yourself being forced to spend your birthday money on ugly shoes, then there may be a way out of it. When you and Mum first go into the store, insist on trying on the shoes you really want, but don't argue when she says that you can't have them because they're not suitable for school. Put the shoes to one side, but make sure that the clerk doesn't put them away. You can achieve this by quickly picking the ugliest shoes you can find.

Put these on and then walk around the store saying "Wow, Mum, I really love *these* shoes. They're much nicer than those other ones. I'm only sad that I haven't got enough money to buy two pairs!" Try to say this in that syrupy sweet way that only kids on American TV shows can really do. If you can also manage to walk in a strange, dream-like fashion, that might help.

You want to give the impression that the shoes have in some way turned you into the Nicest Person in the World, possibly even the Universe. Start to sing with joy — badly, obviously. If you can manage to get a few other customers to run out of the store screaming, so much the better. Mum will probably say:

"Well, if you like them that much, maybe I could pay for a second pair."

The extra pairs of shoes are kept in another room, possibly even the basement. The clerk will not want to leave the store with you behaving like a demented Shirley Temple,[1] and so she'll say:

"Sorry, that's the last pair. But actually, I don't think these are too bad."

At this point she'll pick up the fashion shoes that you originally tried on, in a bustling "Shall I wrap these up? Don't dare say no" sort of way that comes with years of shoestore-clerk training, and bingo! You get the shoes you want, paid for with your own money, and mum (or dad) gets the pleasure of buying you sensible (but ugly) shoes with their own money. Problem solved!

Bribes

What are they?

Bribes are sums of money paid to somebody else in order to get them to do something. Occasionally, they are sums of money paid to somebody in order to get them not to do something, although this is usually called blackmail. Since I haven't done a separate entry on blackmail I'd better quickly cover it here: suppose you'd done something that you didn't want your parents to find out about. In a fit of remorse, when you were feeling

---

1: Shirley Temple was a child star who could kill anyone with sweetness.

weighed down with the burden of guilt, you accidentally told your smaller brother/sister about your "crime," which actually wasn't that serious. Although it might have been; after all, you know what you've done, I don't! Anyway, little brother/sister decides that a very good way to make a bit of cash is to threaten to "tell" unless you cough up so much a week. Horrible or what? Of course, it wouldn't be so bad if you'd thought of it first, but still it is a terrible thing to do to a sibling. After all, you're both on the same side, battling against the alien parent hordes. Anyway, this sort of thing is called blackmail.[1] What you threaten to do to your brother/sister if they ever tell is called attempted murder!

Let's get back to bribery; it's much nicer. There are many, many forms of bribery in society: businessmen give councillors or politicians gifts, holidays, etc., in return for contracts that will make them more cash. Nothing quite like that exists within the bosom of the family. OK, so your parent might say "I'll give you ten bucks if you wash my car".[2] But that could be just a straight business deal.[3] It only really becomes bribery if you just don't want to wash the car. So yes, it's always bribery!

1: Which is neither clever nor funny. It's also illegal; so please don't do it!
2: And pigs might fly.
3: See also JOBS

How to cope

Bribery is a dirty word. So is mud. But it can be turned to your advantage.[1] The big difference between bribery and earnings is that with bribery, the stakes are usually higher. The trick is to make sure that things you are asked to do never become jobs. Jobs have a fixed rate of payment, whereas if you're asked to do something, you can make it seem like a one-off event. But you've got to be clever. The scenario goes something like this:

"Can you give my car a wash?"

"Sorry Dad/Mum/whoever you are. I'm doing my homework."

"No, you're not. You're sitting there doing nothing."

"That's my homework. I've got to see how long I can sit here doing nothing. I'm timing myself."

"We never had anything like that when I was at school."

"No. This is new. It's called social studies. It's replaced corporal punishment as part of the provincial curriculum."

There'll now probably be quite a long pause, while your parents get their heads around the great leaps that education has taken — not always forward, unfortunately — since they were at school. You'll probably hear all this whirring around in your parents' heads. Don't be alarmed. New ideas often settle noisily into adult brains.

1: Bribery can — not mud.

Eventually:

"If you wash the car, I'll give you a twonie."

Note that the goal posts have moved. The Parent now expects the car to be washed — actually washed clean — for two dollars!

"Isn't there a minimum wage?" you think, but don't say. I'll explain why in a minute. Here's how the conversation goes:

"Four dollars. Five."

"Sorry — I'm busy."

"Oh come on, it won't even take five minutes!" (FIVE?!? Two and a half, tops!) " . . . I'll give you ten dollars."

It's at this point that you have to play a very careful game. It's exactly like chess, but without the board or the pieces or the — actually, it's nothing like chess at all. But it is tricky. One of the things you *mustn't* say is:

"Ten bucks? Wow! I'll clean it every week for ten bucks!"

But then you probably realized that!

The best approach is to give a huge sigh, as you appear to break your concentration.

"Oh, well," you sigh, "I'm going to have to start this project all over again! I might as well wash the car. Ten bucks, you said? OK — just this once."

Try to get the money up front. Impossible, I know, but try; because if you don't, then getting the money will be:

a) dependent on how well you do the job, which you already know is going to be *badly*. And . . .

b) impossible.

If your younger sibling comes out while you're washing the car and hangs around asking tricky car-washing related questions, such as "aren't you going to put any water in your bucket?" then this is almost certainly your parent's idea of quality control. Another very good reason for making sure you get the money up front is that otherwise, this will happen:

Yes! Little siblings can be relied on to snitch on you every time. Unless, of course, you bribe them first.

But why do I insist that you should make sure that this is a one-off and not a regular date with a sponge, bucket and car? I would have thought that that was obvious. If you strike a car-washing deal with your parent on a once-a-week-ten-bucks-a-time basis, then:

a) You'll be stuck doing it every week, whether you want to or not.

b) You'll never improve on the price, because your parent will say: "You agreed ten dollars!" and no amount of saying "But that was twenty years ago!" will make any difference.

Bus pass

What is it?

An important part of school life, especially for those of you who go to school by bus, is the bus pass.[1] As the name suggests, it's a pass that allows you to travel on the bus without paying. This is because your bus fare has already been paid by your parents when they paid for the pass. The pass is proof of this payment, in much the same way as a banknote is proof that the bank will give you that amount of precious metal, even though they won't. But unlike a banknote, a bus pass is worth its weight in gold.[2] It's the difference between getting home or being cast into school-kid wilderness, forced to wander forever carrying a very heavy bag, wearing ugly shoes. Try boarding the bus without your pass and see how right I am. Even if the driver knows you personally:

"Hello, Driver."

"Oh hello, Young Child Who I Know Personally. How are you today?"

"Fine — except that I've lost my bus pass."

"But it's me! Young Child Who You Know Personally. I travel on your bus every day."

"Not without a pass you don't! How would it be if I let every Tom, Dick and Harry onto the bus without a pass?"

1: A totally unimportant part of school life for those of you who don't, but stick with it!

2: Actually, bus passes are so light and flimsy that they're probably *literally* worth their weight in gold.

He pauses to greet a few of your schoolmates (and check their passes):

Then he turns to you:

"You still here? Beat it!"

"But how am I going to get home?"

"That's not my problem. You can go by bus if you pay the fare."

"But I've got a bus pass."

"Let's see it."

"I've lost it."

How to cope

The simple answer is: never lose your bus pass. But that's easier said than done. Bus passes are made from a special material that is noted for its lose-ability. A bus pass can be chained to a block of concrete in the glare of searchlights and security cameras, and still disappear. The great magician and escapologist Harry Houdini was made of bus-pass material. David Blaine isn't. None of which solves your problem. Sorry. I suppose all we can hope for is bus drivers who realize that, if a person travels on the bus every day of his life using a bus pass, and then suddenly says "I've lost it," he is probably telling the truth. After all, who in their right mind would want to lie in order to travel on a bus, other than an escaped lunatic?

Maybe the driver thinks he's carrying a load of fare-dodging escaped lunatics! That's worrisome. But even more worrisome is the fact that he doesn't really see you, he only sees the pass; and with that dangerous level of short-sightedness they've put him in charge of a bus! Now that *is* scary!

Cash

What is it?

Well, I think we've established exactly what it is. The reason that I've included it in this A-Z is to remind me to tell you to always insist on cash. Preferably up front. Parents will sometimes try to get you to do things for pieces of cake or an extra half an hour before bedtime.

Take the money; you can buy your own cake, and you never go to sleep when you go to bed, anyway, so half an hour won't mean a thing!

How to cope
Read this book. Simple enough for you?

Counterfeit money

What is it?
Since money was first used, there have always been un-scrupulous people who have tried to forge it. In the early days this was very easy. After all, one shell looked more or less the same as another, as did one feather or one lump of bronze. Who was to say which one was actually money and which one wasn't? This is why lumps of bronze were stamped, so that everyone knew that they were really coins. These days, coins and banknotes are very sophisticated.

The paper that banknotes are printed on carries a water-mark, although why anyone would imagine that drib-bling a bit of water on a banknote would keep some-body from forging it beats me. Ha! Ha! Actually, a water-mark is something inside the paper that can only be seen by holding it up to the light. Some banknotes also carry a very fine strip of metal through them, which also makes them very hard to forge. But people still do it, sometimes very successfully. So much so that many stores, bars, restaurants and even taxis now carry a little detection machine. It's a light that they hold the note under that can tell them that it's counterfeit. You can also get an anti-forgery pen. So, as you can see — forgery doesn't really pay.

How to cope

Since you're unlikely to take up forgery, beyond the odd note to get you out of gym class, there's really nothing to cope with. Although if you are caught with a counterfeit bill, it's another matter. The storeowner treats you as though you actually forged the bill yourself. They say things like:

"Did you know that this ten-dollar bill is counterfeit?"

Surely that has to be the stupidest question ever. If you did know, then presumably you were trying to pass it off as real — in which case you're not likely to admit it, are you? And if you didn't know, are they ever going to believe you? Maybe the only way of coping is to carry your own anti-forgery kit.

Debt

What is it?

If you borrow money that you then can't pay back, you are said to be "in debt." A typical situation that you are likely to find yourself in is this: you're out shopping for something sensible with your parent(s). You see something that is definitely not sensible, but really *cool* and you simply *must* have it.

But you're a bit strapped for cash. In fact, you haven't got any. But you can't let a little thing like no money stop you. After all, it's only twenty-five dollars. So what do you do? You go:

"Mum — can you lend me twenty-five dollars? I'll pay you back."

A bit of a rash promise, I know, but you're desperate.

"All right — but make sure you do."

Wow! This woman is a saint. Can she really be your mum? Anyway, you get the cash, buy the thing, making sure not to wave it about in mum's face too much; after all, she's not likely to appreciate why you think it's so *cool* because she's a parent.

Your joy is complete. It's easy to forget that you are in debt to the tune of twenty-five dollars, and to a woman who never forgets *anything*. Sheesh, she can even tell you which *Guiding Light* character was the first one to have her brain removed.[1] So she's bound to remember something as momentous as lending you money.

How to cope
The first thing to do is never mention the money, ever, not even in passing or as a joke. Comments like: "That's the last you've seen of that twenty-five dollars," are definitely a bad idea. You should be able to tell when Mum is building up to asking for her money back, because parents don't understand subtlety. When you notice this happening, you go into action: start leaving things around the dining room (if you're anything like us, the dining room is probably the kitchen). The sort of thing I'm thinking about is a sock, a magazine, a bit of Lego; things that in themselves are not too noticeable. But after a week of dumping things, quite a pile will have built up, although because it's spread around the room it'll probably be only mildly irritating.

Once you've built up a decent collection, move the whole mess into the middle of the dining-room table and retreat to the bathroom.

1: And not have it replaced with acting talent, unfortunately.

After a very short time you should hear a minor explosion; this will be the sound of your mum reaching the end of her tether. Fix your face in an expression of concern — checking in the bathroom mirror will help you achieve this — and then head downstairs. Stroll into the dining room/kitchen and say:

"Everything all right, Mum? You haven't seen my left sock, have you?"

"If it was on the table, then it's in the garbage."

Change your concerned expression to one of horror as you take in — apparently for the first time — the fact that the entire contents of the dining-room table have disappeared.

"Oh, no!" you cry, confident that an Oscar award is waiting around the corner. "The twenty-five dollars that I owe you was with that stuff!"

A number of things could now happen:

1. Mum could say: "Oh, dear. Well, it's my fault. I'll never see that again." And your debt will be wiped out.
2. Mum may immediately head for the garbage can and start raking through it.

If this happens, then it might be a good idea to start telling her about the project you're doing at school on the Black Death. You could point out the fact that it spread and ultimately killed half of Europe due to the amount of trash lying in the streets and backyards; not to mention kitchen/dining-room tables. That should stop her.

3. It's possible that while you're discussing the problem, the garbage collectors might arrive and take away the offending trash without anyone hearing them. This is very likely; garbage collectors are as nifty as ninjas when it comes to garbage removal. If this happens your mum might say: "Oh well, you did your best to pay me back, dear. It's my own silly fault that I lost the money."

4. The absolute favourite situation is like #3, but instead of mum admitting defeat, she complains very loudly to the public works department, even threatening to tell the local newspapers; even the local TV station.[1] Public works will "refund" the twenty-five dollars, and maybe a little bit more besides, without batting an eyelid. Well, actually they might bat an eyelid, or even two, although flirting is not an essential part of customer relations.

In this last scenario, everybody wins: Mum gets her money, you get to hang on to yours and public works gets to pride itself on its high standard of customer care.

1: You may have to suggest this; Mum will never think of it on her own.

I suppose the only slight down side is that what you would be doing is technically fraud, and therefore illegal.

Dues

What are they?

Dues are something you have to pay to belong to something. Whether it's the Cubs, Brownies, the Canadian Society for the Protection of Birds, or the Mystical Order of the Missing Left Sock,[1] you'll have to pay dues. Incidentally, the Peter Corey Fan Club is free, mainly because it doesn't exist.

Sometimes these have to be paid once a year, which isn't so bad. But some of them are paid every week. This is OK when you're little, because your parents are happy to pay your dues for you; this is their way of encouraging you to go.[2] But as you get older, obviously they're less gung-ho, mainly because there are lots of other things that they have to pay for: school trips, library fines, the next-door neighbour's broken windows, and so on. And so there will come a time when your parents will tentatively suggest:

1: The Mystical Order of the Missing Left Sock doesn't exist, so please don't try to join it.
2: You probably wouldn't be caught dead there, otherwise!

"Maybe you would like to pay your own Scouts dues this week?"

Are they completely *insane*? Surely the words *like* and *pay* are not legally allowed to be in the same sentence, are they? But no, even though your parents probably are, technically speaking, insane (all parents are), in this instance they are totally serious and acting — as far as they are concerned anyway — totally rationally.

How to cope

Of course, the simplest way around this is to give up whatever it is that you're being asked to pay the dues for. It's amazing how quickly things lose their charm when they stop being free. But maybe you don't want to give up this particular activity. Maybe it's fun; or maybe it's a great way to meet members of the opposite sex, in which case it's probably not the Scouts. In my experience, the Scouts was a great way to meet trees, or useful bits of string, but not girls.[1]

Let's just say you happen to want to stay in this particular club or organization, for whatever reason, but simply can't afford it. So what do you do?

There is the straightforward approach: you go to the parent in question and say, "I desperately want to stay in

---

1: Actually I'm lying, but I'm not prepared to go into details!

the Margaret Brainsworthy Memorial Knitting Club, but I just can't afford to."

This approach is honest, wholesome, and to the point. So obviously it's not likely to work because parents do not understand any of these concepts. Therefore, a bit of deception is needed:

A few minutes before you are due to leave the house to attend the Margaret Brainsworthy Memorial Knitting Club (or maybe it's the WigglyBum Freeform Dance Ensemble), you walk into the room, clearly not ready to go.

"Aren't you going this week?" asks Concerned Parent.

"Nah. I thought I'd give it a miss."

"But I thought you really enjoyed it."

At this point there are a number of routes the conversation can take. I will outline two of them:

ROUTE A:

"Yes, I do love it — it's the best thing ever. But I just can't afford the dues."

Because you are delivering this bombshell so close to the time that you would normally need to leave the house, the parent does not really have time fully to assess the implications of what you are saying, beyond the fact that you want to go, can't afford it, and are clearly upset. To be honest, anything more complicated than that would probably be beyond their comprehension anyway; they are adults after all. Their most likely response is:

"Let's talk about it later. If I drop you off in the car, we might just make it. And don't worry about the dues — I'll take care of those."

Of course, not all parents are this shallow. There are some parents who are frankly so devious that they should be banned by law from being parents in the first place. For this type of parent a more convoluted route is needed:

ROUTE B:
"Do you want the truth?" (A sure cue for a lie!) "I only ever joined [NAME OF CLUB] because you wanted me to. I know that you were the champion knitter/top dancer/niftiest ninja when you were my age, and I was trying to be as good as you."

"So it's not a question of money, then?"

At this point don't say: "Of course not."

After all, it *is* a question of money, and you need to make sure that money stays in the frame. So play the money down, but don't blow it out, as in:

"Weeeeellllll . . . Not entirely."

Guilt will kick in. For the parent, not for you! This is surprising, I admit, but parents are not totally impervious to guilt, even though most other emotions are a complete mystery to them. The result of the guilt will be something along the lines of:

"Well, obviously you'll never be quite as good as me because you've got your father's knees/mother's teeth;[1] but you can't give up. What if *I* paid for you to go?"

"Great! Any chance I could get a ride, too?"

DON'T PUSH IT!

1: They always blame the other parent.

Earnings

See JOBS

Errands

What are they?

An errand is usually when you go somewhere for someone. To the store when one of your parents has run out of something, for instance.

"Oh, no! There's no jam! Run up the corner store for me, would you?"

This is, of course, a great opportunity to practise your bribery skills.

"Sure I *would*, but I need to clean my school shoes."

In this instance, you have to be sure that cleaning your shoes was not something that you'd told your parents that you'd already done the night before. But it has to be said that most parents are particularly gullible when it comes to things like clean shoes:

Even if they don't approve, no parent likes to think that they're out of fashion; it's a sign of old age.[1]

1: Of course, what they don't realize is that when you actually *do* get old you don't give a hoot about fashion. Not that I'd know about that; I'm far too young!

The problem with errands is that they usually involve words like "run" and "pop." By which I mean that they are fast things; things done in a hurry. And like most things done in a hurry, there's not a lot of room for negotiation. So long-winded and subtle ploys are out of the question.

How to cope

Listen out for phrases like "You can keep the change." These are the key to a successful errand. Of course, a bit of nudging might be required; even a blatant "can I keep the change?" although that might be too obvious. No, probably not — after all, we are talking about parents, aren't we? They're not noted for being able to see through a ruse, even though they were once young themselves.[2] Having extracted the key phrase by whatever method (try "Did you say 'keep the change?'" — that might work), you head off to the store. Now if you want to make the maximum profit out of the trip, you return with only half the things on the list; this whole venture was thrown together in a blind panic, so you can be forgiven for not remembering everything.

Or you could try the "they didn't have any" ploy. But be careful:

2: Hard to believe, I know — but it was only once. Probably a Thursday.

"Where's my newspaper?"

"They didn't have any."

"But they're a newsstand!"

Yes! Be careful! Now comes the moment of truth:

"Where's my change?"

"You told me to keep it."

"Oh, yeah."

Again, be careful; coming back from the store having bought nothing, and then expecting to keep the change, is probably pushing it, just a bit. But then again, you know your own parents better than I do.

Exchange rates

What are they?

If you travel outside the country, you have to change your money. This is because different countries use different coins. Part of the fun of going abroad, usually on vacation or for a school trip, is having different coins in your pocket. The more you travel, the more you realize just how boring the money is in this country. Yes! Foreign money is much more fun. Until you try to spend it! The first big problem is figuring out how much everything costs. Oh yes, you've been told that 234 dublonkies is worth fifty-seven cents, but do you really want to be doing a major mathematical calculation every time you want to buy a bag of chips?

ARE YOU SURE THIS IS RIGHT? I COULD BUY A SMALL HOUSE WITH THIS BACK HOME!

The other problem is that, if you're on a school trip, you want your friends to think that you're well travelled and have a reasonable command of the local currency. And that's the biggest problem.

How to cope
You can, of course, try always paying with a banknote. The problems with this are:

a) you might be handing over a thousand-dollar bill for something that costs fifty cents. And . . .

b) you're almost certainly going to wind up with a mountain of small coins, so much so that you won't be able to walk.

So how do you cope? Go into the store with confidence, pick up the thing you want to buy and take it to the counter. Remember, you are not trying to impress the storeowner. This is impossible anyway, because she already knows that you're a tourist; the tacky tourist baseball cap is a bit of a giveaway[1], not to mention your total lack of command of the local language. But you do want to impress your friends/family. So you pull out a handful of coins and start pretending to count them out with the speed and accuracy of a native. As you do this, drop a couple and then say: "These coins are so fiddly! Here — help yourself!" So saying, you toss the handful of coins onto the counter. If you can accompany this

1: Giveaway? You're joking! It cost thirty dollars! Or rather, 2000.7 dublonkies.

action with a bit of gibberish, your friends will probably think you're talking the local language, even though the storeowner won't. The storeowner will help herself to the right money, you'll scoop up the change and everything will be fine. As long as the storeowner is honest. If she isn't, then you really might end up paying two thousand bucks for a bag of chips!

NOTE: you can buy currency converters that figure out the exchange rate for you. The only thing is that if you're clever enough to work one of those, you're clever enough to do it in your head!

Finders Keepers

What is it?

It's an expression that means if you find something you should be allowed to keep it. Of course, sometimes the thing you find isn't actually lost. A horse wandering along the road, for instance, might not actually be lost; it might just have seen a gate open and gone for a walk. Besides, would you really want to keep a great big horse, especially when cleaning out the mouse cage is such a pain every week? Of course, money is different. A dollar coin lying around on the floor is very inviting. You pick it up, call out "finders keepers!" and as far as you're concerned you are a dollar better off and that's that.

Unfortunately, it's usually just the beginning.

"Did you find some money?" asks Dad.

"Yes," you innocently reply.

"Well, if it's got the Queen's head on it, it's mine."

"No it's not! It's *my* twonie!" pipes up Little Brother.

"It's only a dollar," you point out. "So it can't be yours!"

"Yes! That's half of it!"

And so begins the worst family feud since Aunt Mabel died and left her teeth in her will.

Anyway, back to the loonie. Mum has now joined the lineup of claimants. Your big sister has brought along a lawyer, who is trying to explain the laws of treasure trove, which up until now have never actually been applied to a dropped loonie. Your chances of hanging on to your new-found "fortune" are quickly slipping away.

How to cope

If you see a coin, do the following in this order:

1. Pick it up.
2. Shut up about it.

If somebody has lost it and they ask you about it, you can always say: "Yes, I've got it. I put it in my pocket for safekeeping." If you start asking around to try and find the owner, you'll discover that everyone within a 30-kilometre radius has lost it. Of course, if you find a wallet stuffed with credit cards and cash and stuff, you should take it straight to the nearest police station. If you ask around, you'll discover again that, amazingly, everyone has just lost their wallet.

Funds

What are they?

The term "funds" can mean several things. It can mean money, as in the bank manager writing to tell you that you have insufficient funds in your account.[1] It can also mean something that has been set up to raise money for something, such as the *Save the Lifeboat Fund*. Or the *Rebuild the Church Spire Fund*. Or the *Feed the Rabbit Fund*. Yes! I think I've just hit on a great money-making scheme. After all, one of the greatest expenses is feeding your pet, isn't it? All that hard-earned allowance going into the bottomless pit known as Bunnikins. But if you were to set up a fund to help feed him, that would take the pressure off your already overstretched purse strings.

Of course, there are snags, as you might imagine. People are unlikely to give you money to feed your rab-

---

1: Which is bank-speak for broke.

bit. After all, they've probably got rabbits of their own
. . . or should!

How to cope
Well, of course, you can't. Forget I ever mentioned it. A
rabbit-feeding fund is a silly idea — unless *you* can make
it work!

Gift certificate

What is it?
This is a form of money. But, unlike other forms, you can
only buy something from the store it came from.
Although it is commonly known as a gift certificate, its
full name is "Oh, no! What can I get them for
Christmas/birthday? I know, I'll give them a gift certificate." Although, in fairness, it has to be said that many
people like getting them as presents. But suppose that
you've been given a gift certificate for your birthday or
Christmas, but you don't want to buy something from
that store. Or more to the point, there's something you
want much, much more, but no amount of hinting has
managed to get the idea through to any of your relatives.[1]
So instead of the latest *Great Pink Wobbly Things* CD —
which is awesome if you like middle-of-the-road hip hop
— or the latest PC game *Clam Throbbing Beats Off the
Graphically Challenged Alien Hordes Single-handedly III*
— which is also awesome if you like blood-spattered
body parts and ballerinas — you open up your birthday
card and get — wow! — a bookstore gift certificate!

How to cope
So how do you turn this limited currency into hard cash,

1: Don't worry — relatives have this problem. It's called selective deafness and
it usually means that they don't want you to have it.

without offending anyone? Well, you could try saying: "Oh, a bookstore gift certificate! Great! But I think I've already got one." You could try that, but it's unlikely to work. If you're an identical twin and your twin has been given cash then you could try saying to your twin: "I think this is for you. People are always getting us mixed up." This is also unlikely to work.

If you can't actually con anyone into exchanging it for money, then your best hope is to find another store — one that sells CDs and computer games and also books. Then, what you do is use your gift certificate to buy a book at the store that issued the gift certificate. You then take the book into the other store, and say:

"A relative bought this for me as a present, but I've already got it. Can I exchange it for a different one?"

"Of course you can," beams the clerk.

"Thank you," you reply.

Then you have a quick look around at their (very unimpressive) book selection. You then go back to the clerk.

"Hmm," you say, looking glum, "you don't appear to have any book that I could allow myself to be seen reading. I wonder if I could have a refund?"

"Uh, hmm," stammers the assistant, quietly thinking that making this difficult decision could be more than his job is worth.

"I know," you say helpfully. "I could take a computer game instead, even though I'd much rather have a book, you understand."

"Of course!" blurts out the relieved clerk.

You select your game and go back to the counter.

"I'll take this one. Maybe I could have it a bit cheaper, since I don't really want it and will probably never play it."

No! I think we could be pushing our luck!

Going "Dutch"

What is it?

Well for a start, it's not putting on wooden shoes and talking about tulips; it means sharing the cost of something.

This is great if you're on a date and you know that it's likely to cost you more than you've actually got. Nothing jumps into the path of true love and makes a totally scary face faster than lack of cash. But the going-Dutch-ness of the date has to be established before the date starts. It's no good taking your date to a fancy restaurant,[1] then saying as the bill arrives: "Your half comes to $15.75." This is not on the Top-Ten List of Ways to Impress Your Date. Neither is saying: "You pay the bill while I go to the can, and I'll settle up with you later."

1: OK — McDonald's.

How to cope

As you might imagine, going Dutch is a tricky business. One way to establish it is to be totally honest, and say: "I'd really like to go to the movies with you, but I'm a bit short of cash. How about going Dutch?" That instantly gets rid of anyone who's after your fortune. Unfortunately, there's an unwritten law of human nature that says that the ones that like you for all the wrong reasons are the ones *you* like the most.

If you don't feel brave enough to go for the direct approach, then plan B is probably your best option: make sure you've got enough cash on you to pay for the evening, just in case things go terribly wrong. Beg off your brothers and sisters, if you really must, but don't make the fatal mistake of going into detail about why you need the cash. They'll tease you forever if you do! Once fully armed with plenty of dough, meet your date and proceed to the movie theatre.

At the box office, check the price of the tickets and then fumble in your pockets. *Don't say*: "Can my friend get in for half price, since he/she's not very tall?" That would not be wise; it would be dumb, in fact. Of course, if you want to go for *TOTALLY STUPID*, you could say: "If we start making out and miss some of the movie, can we have a partial refund?" That will guarantee that the evening won't cost you a penny, because your date will disappear as fast as light, or even faster. It's better not to say anything.

Also, you must not look as though you're desperately searching for cash. It's better that everyone thinks that you're so used to carrying great wads of the stuff that your pockets are the size of a small South American country. During this "performance," your date may do one of a number of things:

1. Say: "Here, let me get the tickets." To which you *do not* reply "I was hoping you'd say that," even if you're thinking it. Try saying something like: "That's very kind of you to offer. We could split it, if you like."

2. Your date may just stand there and watch you. In which case you have to pull your money out, pay up and look forward to several months working as your sibling's personal slave.

Of course, the more daredevil among you might want to opt for the following ploy: Make a counterfeit $100 bill. They're brown, I think. I once heard someone talk about one and I think he said that they were brown. Wave this at the box-office cashier and say: "Sorry, I don't have anything smaller." The cashier will refuse to change it, partly because she'll assume that it's a forgery (and she'd be right) and partly because she won't believe that it's your money (and she'd be right again — it isn't *anybody's* money! It isn't even *money!*).

Your date, assuming that you're loaded, will offer to pay for the tickets. Once inside the theatre you go to the bathroom and "lose" your $100 bill. You come back to your seat and explain, saying something like: "I've just been robbed in the bathroom by a daring gang of international $100-bill thieves, who deftly made their escape through a tiny skylight to a waiting helicopter. We could chase after them on our bikes, but they'll probably be miles away by now."

Try to be subtle about it, obviously. You then produce your *actual* money and say: "I've still got $11.71. So I'll be able to treat us to something to eat later."

"We'll split it," pipes up your date, almost as though programmed. Problem solved.

All right — one ploy. And not a very good one, at that. Sorry.

"Going rate", The

What is it?

The going rate is an expression that refers to the cost or value of something. For instance, the going rate for washing a car might be fifteen dollars. It *might* be, but you're likely never to get it![1] The going rate is important when

---

1: If your parents will pay fifteen dollars for a car wash, drop me a line and I'll pop over and do it. Although I might have to charge travel expenses on top, so it could work out to be expensive (with any luck!).

you're negotiating a price for any job your parents want you to do. Yes, I know I said earlier that you should try to avoid getting hooked into doing regular jobs, because that makes it very difficult to negotiate a pay raise. But sometimes it's unavoidable, especially if you've got brothers or sisters who are just waiting to take the job from you. This also makes the going rate very hard to negotiate, because whatever price you suggest, they'll be prepared to do it cheaper.

How to cope

The first thing to establish is that you're the best person for the job, because in business, the cheapest is not necessarily the best. Take car washing, for example: you need to convince the parent involved that they not only want their car clean, but they also want it to *stay* clean, at least until it gets dirty again. Yes — I know that doesn't make sense, but don't worry, adults never notice things like that. They'll probably be prepared to pay a bit more for the reassurance that the job will be well done.[1] Having established a fair price,[2] then wash the car exceptionally well, inside and out. Depending on your bribery skills, you may be able to get somebody else to do this for you. Then invite your parent to examine your handiwork. It helps, at this point, if you can arrange for a few passersby to . . . uh, pass by and admire your efforts. You

1: Although don't hold your breath!
2: I.e. ridiculously high.

can probably pick up a few willing old people at the local seniors' home. After all, they like to feel useful and they don't get out much. Get them to walk by and say something like: "New car, Mr. Phillips?" or whatever your parent's name is.

A few words of warning here:

a) Don't get them all to pass by together and chorus their comments; a small group of shuffling old lunatics, all speaking together, just might give the game away.

b) Make sure that they don't actually say: "New car, Mr. Phillips?" unless it's your dad they're talking to, and that's his name. Again, this can be a bit of a giveaway.

Having established that you are far and away the best car washer in the neighbourhood (if not exactly the cheapest) you need to make the job pay. The first thing you need to do is to make sure that the payment is secure, whatever happens. This should be fairly easy, since it's just a question of establishing that you'll clean the car on a given day and get a fixed amount for doing it, with no strings attached. Once you've got this straightened out, the next stage in the operation is to reduce the amount of time you have to spend cleaning the car. Carefully study the weather reports and try to arrange to clean the car just as a storm is breaking out. Your parent will insist that you abandon the cleaning for fear of you dying of pneumonia, and will still pay you as long as you point out that you would have finished washing the car if they hadn't stopped you. Always try to put the blame for the job not being completed on your parent; *never* be the one to suggest that you should stop. Once you've got this regular job firmly established, you may even be able to persuade your little brother to wash the car for you — for a fraction of the money that you get paid.

This is called sub-contracting, which basically means that you get somebody else to do it, and you pocket most of the dough. This is always a good idea, because if your little brother makes a disaster of the job — which he almost certainly will — you can blame him, which means that he'll never be in a position to steal the job away from you.

I.O.U.

What is it?
When people borrow money from each other, they sometimes sign a slip of paper saying: "I.O.U. (or I Owe You) the sum of X amount, signed . . . " And if you're lucky, they'll actually sign it! You've probably opened up

your piggy bank and found a scrap of paper in there saying "I.O.U. $10", at which point you instantly know that one of your parents has been raiding your piggy bank again. Unfortunately, most parents "forget" to sign the note, so it isn't always easy to tell who's "borrowed" it. Getting it back is even harder!

This is a tough one, because unless you know which parent dug in and left the I.O.U., it's tricky to insist that they repay you. Logic might tell you that the fact that they've left an I.O.U. in the first place is proof of their intention to repay the money. But you're old enough to have realized that "logic" and "parents" don't mix.

How to cope
As you will know, I don't usually suggest persuading your brother or sister to help you, mainly because I know from experience that this rarely works. But in some situations it's the only solution; and this is just such a situation. Tell your brother/sister that your cash would be a lot safer if you stored it in each other's piggy banks. Obviously, get them to swear on pain of death, or something even worse, that they will never touch your money (or even sniff it, for that matter). Having made this pact your money will now be safely in their piggy bank in their bedroom, while their money will be in your piggy bank in your bedroom. With me so far? Good! At this

point it might help things if you boast openly, in front of your parents, about the vast amount of money you've managed to save. This ensures that if they go searching for emergency milk money, they are far more likely to dip into the piggy bank in your room than in anyone else's. Thus whenever they "borrow" money they'll actually be borrowing your brother/sister's money, not yours!

Obviously you'll need to back your sibling up (ever so slightly) when they attempt to get the "borrowed" money back, but only because you may need them in the (unlikely) event of it ever happening to you.

Jobs

What are they?

You'll be pleased to hear that they've made shoving eight-year-olds up chimneys illegal,[1] but kids *can* get a paper route. Paper routes have always been traditionally the way teenagers first start to scrape a decent amount of money together. Billions of bikes have been paid for with paper routes. I think I got my first "real" bike by doing a paper route. By "real" I mean with tons of gears and accessories. I also worked for the milkman — delivering milk, not surprisingly. The great thing about this sort of

1: Unless, of course, you have an eight-year-old sibling.

job is that it brings in more cash than running errands for Mum and Dad. You are also definitely going to get paid, whereas Mum and Dad will do everything that they possibly can to wriggle out of paying you. But newspapers *have* to pay you, or they get into trouble. Unfortunately, this kind of job involves getting up very early and going out in every kind of weather.

THERE HAS GOT TO BE AN EASIER WAY TO MAKE A LIVING!

It isn't something you can do only when you feel like it. People need their paper, usually before they go to work. My paper carrier delivers at four o'clock in the morning! Mind you, he is a bit loopy.

How to cope

Obviously, getting up really, really early and tramping around the streets delivering newspapers is not everybody's idea of fun, even if it does bring in extra money. So the problem is how to earn a paper carrier's wage without putting yourself through too much extremely dangerous exercise. Hmmm . . . it's a tricky one. I may need to go and make a snack and think about it. Back in a minute. Maybe you'd like to read on while I do that.

Kiss-o-grams

What are they?

Anyone who's ever been to their older brother/sister's birthday party (even if they were there in disguise) will know that one of the worst things about getting older is that so-called friends spring surprises on you. And one of the popular surprises at the moment is a kiss-o-gram. A total stranger turns up on your doorstep dressed as Tarzan, Tinky Winky or Elvis Presley.[1]

The person who opened the door lets them in, for some strange reason, and they proceed to kiss the person whose birthday it is. This sort of thing also happens at weddings, anniversaries and funerals, although it's usually less successful at funerals — I can't imagine why. Kiss-o-grams are hideous in every way and deeply embarrassing.

GOING TO A COSTUME PARTY?

NO. A FUNERAL

1: Actually, if somebody turns up on your doorstep dressed as Elvis, it probably really is Elvis. He isn't dead, you know! Ask anybody!

How to cope

Just avoid them. But why am I telling you about kiss-o-grams in a book about cash? Well, it suddenly occurred to me that they're a good way of making money.

Now, before you start shouting: "No way! I'm not tramping around the neighbourhood in costume, in every kind of weather! I'd rather have a paper route!"[1] — I wasn't seriously suggesting that you did that. I was thinking more about a sort of non-kiss-o-gram, which entails you *threatening* to kiss people unless they give you money. A word of warning: don't try this on your Auntie Doreen, the one with the beard; she'll kiss anyone. Believe me — I *know*!

Loans

What are they?

In simple terms, they are sums of money that you borrow from somebody. Somebody like a relative. Unfortunately, borrowing from anyone who knows you can be very complicated. Just try borrowing some cash from your sister/brother and see what happens!

1: I still haven't solved the paper route problem, by the way. But I will! Maybe.

How to cope

Don't do it! You already know that if you lend somebody money, it gives you the upper hand. I've already explained elsewhere in the book that having your parents owe you money can be a useful tool in your struggle to get your own way. But if the situation were reversed . . . point taken?

Owing money

See DEBT

Pet costs

What are they?

Pets are wonderful, aren't they? Especially rabbits. I love rabbits, although I couldn't eat a whole one. Only joking! But one thing that pets do (apart from smell) is cost money. OK, so *you* might not have to cough up to own one — parents have a knack of buying you a gerbil when you've asked for a bike — but in the long run, you'll be made to pay.

"Well, it's a lot like a bike," says Mum/Dad/Annoying Relative as they hand over the present. "You still have to clean it every week." Yes, but you can't ride a gerbil, unless you've got extremely short legs. And you don't have to feed a bike.[1]

Gerbils are an entirely different thing. You now find yourself the proud owner of the only gerbil that does nothing but eat. And eat and eat. It has no hobbies. It won't play in its wheel, or with any of its toys. Not that it's actually got a wheel or toys. Well, you can't afford any extras, once you've paid for food every week. And then there's the natural consequence of overeating.

THIS IS MY PET GERBIL

1: You don't even have to clean it if you've got a smaller brother/sister who has a guilty secret, but that's another matter!

You know what I'm talking about. Arthur (as you've named your gerbil, for some strange reason) needs cleaning out every day. And bedding isn't cheap. By the time you've finished paying just to keep your pet *alive*, you've gone through all your allowance, odd-job money, Little Brother Protection Money and anything else that comes your way via bribery (nasty), blackmail (even worse) or any other foul but worthwhile money-making scheme.

How to cope

This is a tricky one, because pets have feelings, too; hard to believe, I know, but true, apparently. So your lack of money shouldn't really reflect on them. Why should they starve, just because your parents are too mean to give you enough allowance? However, the simple fact of the matter is that you just don't have enough dough to feed and care for your pet as well as buy your own essentials, like candy and magazines, and save up for the latest computer game, *Mindless Violence with a Ridiculous-Looking Gun IV*.

Which is where your parents come in. Encourage your parents to be involved in the development of your pet. OK, so most pets just sit there looking bored, but your parents can get involved in that as well.

Perhaps you could even get books from the library on your chosen pet. *The Gerbil: A Friend for Life*; that would be a good one to get. *101 Things To Do with a Dead Rodent* wouldn't. Toss casual "interesting" facts about your pet into the conversation.[1] *DO NOT AT ANY POINT* ever say: "I wanted a bike, but you bought me this useless gerbil," even if you're thinking it; even if the gerbil's thinking it too.

If you don't overdo this, your parent should soon develop a keen interest in your pet. Telltale signs that your scheme is working will be comments from them along the lines of: "I see Arthur has been to the bathroom this morning."[2] Comments like this mean that your parent is hooked, well and truly. It shouldn't take long; after all, parents are simple-minded creatures who don't get out much, so the toilet habits of your pet will be totally awe-inspiring for them. Once you're sure that your parent has the best interests of your pet at heart, you can start saying things like: "Arthur's really wonderful, but I would like to do more for him, like feed him regularly. But I'm on a really tight budget." Then wait for the magic words:

"Well, maybe I could help out."

"How?" you ask, all wide-eyed and innocent.

"Well, perhaps I could chip in with the occasional bag of food or bale of straw."

Then you move in for the kill: "How occasional? What about every Thursday?"

And then I think you'll find that your problem is — as they say — *solved*!

1: This is also a handy way of changing the subject, if you think that your parent is about to tell you off.
2: Of course, it might not actually have been this morning. It might not in fact have been this *week* — it depends on how often you clean the thing out!

Piggy bank

What is it?

It's a container that you keep your money in. It doesn't have to be shaped like a pig. It might be cunningly disguised as My Little Pony, with a large slot between its buttocks where you poke in your allowance, or something in less good taste, but it's still just a box where you keep your money. And as such, it can easily find itself prey to parents with poor housekeeping skills, or siblings with light fingers.

How to cope
Keep it locked. Double locked. Triple locked. And hire a guard dog. Maybe even a private security firm.

Relatives

What are they?
They're not there to humiliate you by trying to kiss you, ruffle your hair or knit you horrible sweaters; they can be a useful source of extra cash. But they have to be approached with caution.

In my experience, aunts and uncles are usually good for a buck or two. This is largely due to the fact that they are your parents' brothers and sisters, and so there's a certain amount of rivalry about trying to appear more generous than your parents are. They needn't worry: *everybody* appears more generous than parents, without making any effort at all.

Grannies and granddads are also a handy source of extra money, except that most of them haven't quite caught up with inflation,[1] so they still think that there are things that exist that only cost a nickel.

WANT AN ICE-CREAM CONE?

YES, PLEASE

HERE'S 25¢, GET EVERYBODY ONE

1: Inflation is the rate at which prices rise and fall. Well, rise anyway!

The biggest problem with relatives is that many of them don't visit that often, so you have to make the most of this rare money-making opportunity.

How to cope
There are various strategies that you can employ in order to capitalize on a visit from a relative.

Because there's probably a certain element of relatives trying to outdo your parents, it's a good idea to try to plant the idea into the visiting relatives' minds that your mum or dad has just been very generous to you. Aunts and uncles usually get taken in by this fairly easily.

But how do you do it? Remember that timing is everything. It may be that your uncle (or aunt) always presses a twonie into your hand on the way *out*, in which case you've probably got plenty of time to work on them. You can do this by getting out an expensive-looking toy and playing with it under their nose; or in the case of a CD, tape, video or computer game, start playing it loudly. This could be something you received as a birthday or Christmas present, or even something you've borrowed from a friend, just for the occasion. Once you've got their attention, they will say something like:

You could also throw in a quick "it cost a fortune" for good measure, but it's best not to overdo it.

A few words of warning here:

1. Make sure it *is* actually expensive (twenty-five dollars or more).
2. Make sure that it isn't something that they bought you.[1] This may seem obvious, but you'd be amazed at how often you can get caught out in this way.
3. Oh — and don't do this in front of your parents, especially if they actually *haven't* played any part in you obtaining the particular item. Parents are notorious for saying: "No, I didn't!" and blowing your scam. This is amazing because in most other ways parents are incredibly good at taking the credit for things they've played no part in — like your upbringing, education, etc.

Having established the (supposed) generosity of your parents, leave your relative to ponder this. Just before they are about to leave, they will almost certainly press enough cash into your hand to buy the toy, CD, tape, etc. several times over. They leave happy in the knowledge that they have outdone their brother/sister/child (i.e. your mum or dad) yet again. You then need to hire an armed guard to accompany you to the mall!

Of course, some relatives are in the habit of pressing a coin into your hand as they arrive. This is because they can't wait to demonstrate how much more generous they are than your parents. In order to draw attention to themselves they make a real show out of slipping you a dollar coin and saying in a very loud whisper: "Don't spend it all at once!" They then do a wink so large that it makes them look like they've got some terrible eye disorder. But how do you turn this sad-and-lonely dollar

1: See also THANK YOU LETTERS

116

coin into a much larger banknote? It isn't easy, but you could try this:

Have a $20 bill folded in the palm of your hand. As they walk away smugly, having given you the dollar coin, you unfold the $20 bill, hold it up in the air for all to see and say very loudly: "Wow! A twenty! Thanks a million!"

Your relative will be astonished that their rather sad little gift of a dollar has miraculously turned into a big fat twenty — unless you're a member of the Society of Canadian Magicians, in which case they'll just think that you're showing off.[1]

"Gosh! Is it?" they'll say.

And now you go in for the kill:

"Oh no!" you say. "THIS IS THE ONE MY MUM GAVE ME EARLIER!"

Said relative will bluster, blush, and (hopefully) dip their hand in their pocket and produce more cash.

A POINT TO REMEMBER:

You should not really expect relatives to give you money every time they come over. Although, why else would they be there?

1: In which case, this ploy won't work for you, I'm afraid. Sorry.

Sales tax

What is it?

This a special tax that is added to the cost of most things that you buy. Electrical things, like personal stereos, computer game consoles, and so on, all have sales tax added to them. CDs and books do too — so if you've bought this book, you've paid the tax. If you've borrowed this book from the library, you won't have had to pay anything, except a huge library fine when you forget to take it back. And since the fine will almost certainly be more than the original cost of the book, you'd be better off buying the book in the first place.

Clothes also have sales tax added on. This explains your parents' reaction to you growing, because every time you grow into another size, they're paying through the nose. And the bigger you get, the more expensive the clothes are.

How to cope

Stay short and use the library (maybe). Although this won't help you get that computer game that you're so desperate for. Unfortunately, there's really no way around the dreaded sales tax, so if you do want something that has tax added, you're going to have to use the skills explained elsewhere in the book, and don't mention the price!

Thank-you letters

What are they?

Letters to relatives, friends of your parents, etc., who have sent you gifts at Christmas or birthday time. They are also a *pain*! And what are they all about? After all, when you give somebody something, do you expect a letter of thanks? Every time you feed your gerbil, do you rush to the mailbox, expecting a badly scrawled thank-you note signed with a paw print?

IS THAT A THANK-YOU NOTE FROM YOUR GERBIL?

NO. IT'S A COMPLAINT. APPARENTLY IT WANTS BETTER-QUALITY FOOD!

Of course you don't! You give, with no thought of reward. But what you have to remember is that adults are different, in case you hadn't noticed. They positively *bathe* in gratitude. Which is why, every time they slip you a loonie when nobody's looking, they make sure that the whole world sees them do it. If that doesn't sound as though it makes sense, it's because these are adults we're talking about. You'll probably find that they keep your thank-you notes in a scrapbook. Actually, they don't, of course; some adults don't even read them. It would probably be a good idea to find out which adults read the notes and which don't. That way you'll know whether or not you have to worry about tricky stuff like spelling.

Whether they read them or not, *not* sending a thank-you letter can seriously affect your chances of getting anything half decent next time.

How to cope

The most boring thing about thank-you letters is thinking of things to say to people that you hardly know/hardly like/hate with a passion. Close relatives are not so difficult, because you probably have more in common with them. This is just as well, because relatives that you see regularly are far more likely to keep hinting about not getting a letter.

Actually, the people who hassle you the most when it comes to thank-you letters are parents; so they are the ones you need to impress. Most parents are not happy to let you write your thank-you letters on your computer. They feel that the sincerity of the "thank you" is in some way weakened by it being in type. This is just one of the many mysteries of the adult brain. Frankly, the only way most of your relatives will ever be able to *read* the letter is if it's printed! This is quite a useful argument to use when trying to persuade your parents that the letters would be better written on the PC, but don't overdo it or they may arrange for you to have private handwriting lessons. A much better argument is the one that goes:

"If I do them on the computer, then I can scan in pictures of the family, the dog's boil and loads of other interesting stuff."

You might even be able to persuade other members of the family to add their own parts, so that a boring thank-you letter becomes a really "interesting" family newsletter. This should work extremely well, although you will need a computer, printer, scanner and all the necessary software. Have you got all that? No? Oh well, you'd better get writing then![1]

Ugly shoes

What are they?

Imagine the situation: you've been given some birthday money. You've seen these amazing shoes in the window, and you've been drooling over them for weeks. Maybe you've even told your parents. And maybe, in a rash moment, they've even said: "Well, you can buy those with your birthday money, when it's your birthday." You go into the store, having managed to give your parents the slip. Yes! The shoes are still in the window! You tell the clerk what you want, and he says "back in a minute" and disappears into the bowels of the store. He then returns with the most startling array of disgustingly ugly shoes that you've ever seen in your life.

ARE THESE SHOES OR THE BOXES THEY COME IN?

1: Use your thank-you letter to tell the various relatives that you are saving up for a computer, scanner, printer, etc. That way it's not a wasted opportunity.

You tentatively say:

"What about the ones in the window?"

"They're in the window, I'm afraid."

"Yes. Can I have those?"

"No."

"Why not?"

"Because they're in the window."

"Well, can't you get them out?"

"No."

"Why not?"

"Because they've been super-glued in, in case some-body tries to steal them."

"What about if somebody tries to *buy* them?"

"Buy them?"

This is said as though the mere idea that anyone would want to go into a shoe store and buy shoes is just too bizarre to contemplate.

How to cope

You can't. Sorry. It's just one of those horrible facts of life that if you go into a shoe store you will come out with ugly shoes, whether your parent is with you or not.

In fact, you might be better off if you take a parent with you and adopt the scam outlined under "Birthday money." You might, but can you really be seen in public with either of your parents? That could be much, much worse than being seen in public in ugly shoes!

Vacation money

What is it?

We talked about this at length earlier, but what I never did was explain any strategies for avoiding the vacation money problems that I'd outlined. So I'll do it now.

How to cope

The trickiest thing about vacation is hanging on to your cash and spending it on the kind of good times that you promised yourself while you were struggling to scrape the money together. But this strategy will help:

A few days before the vacation, work yourself into a state of panic. Watching *Dawson's Creek* should help — it's full of teenagers in a state of panic, so you should easily be able to find a role model.

TOO LITTLE   TOO MUCH   JUST RIGHT

Having achieved the right level of distraught child, head off to your parents and tell them, as tearfully as possible, that your carefully gathered vacation money has disappeared. There's no real need to go into details. You don't, for example, need to invent a tale about standing there helpless while it spontaneously combusted. The mere fact that you are beside yourself with grief will be enough to persuade your parents that you have a problem. They won't want you to grieve too long; they can't really handle emotions.[1] "Don't worry about it,"

1: Their own or other people's.

they'll say. "We'll make sure you have spending money on vacation."

This is actually the last thing you want, but don't worry, I'll show you the way around it. If your parents insist on paying, since you've got no money, you just opt for the most expensive of everything. You'll soon have them refusing to bankroll you. Your siblings will come in handy at this point, because they can always be relied on to point out that it isn't fair that your parents are paying for you, when *they* have to use their own money. Pretty soon, your family will be happy to leave you back at the hotel — struggling to complete the hotel's only jigsaw puzzle, which has most of its pieces missing; or playing Scrabble with the hotel owner's deaf and dyslexic granny.

Once the family has gone off to do family things, you can take yourself and your money out for a day of real excitement. A couple of words of warning, though: always make sure that you know roughly what time your family will be returning to the hotel, and *never* boast to your brothers and sisters about the fabulous time you're having, because they'll almost certainly squeal to Mum and Dad. Or, even worse than that, they'll insist on coming with you!

Wages

What are they?

Most jobs result in a salary, or wage. This is a sum of money paid either weekly or monthly in return for you doing a job. Some of you will have paper routes and so you'll already know roughly, what wages are all about. They should really be called WAGESL, standing for Working And Getting Ever So Little, because, frankly, wages for the kind of jobs that you are allowed to do are not that good. They also have none of the "perks" that jobs have in the adult world.[1]

Take a paper route, for instance. Do you get more money if it's raining or snowing? Of course not! Does the company provide special clothing to protect against wind, rain, snow, large dogs and rabid hamsters? Of course they don't! But if you were an adult, you'd not only have all this supplied with the job, but you'd also get bonuses, sick leave, maternity leave, a pension, a company car and all sorts of other things that almost make the job worth doing. Almost, but not quite.

How to cope

I have said elsewhere in the book that you should try to avoid fixed rates for jobs around the house because it's often very difficult (i.e. impossible) to get the rate improved once it's been set. Remember that these rates are set by parents, and parents don't understand things like inflation. Also, I'm thinking in terms of wages not being something you earn for doing a particular job, but more an amount that you get on top of your allowance for doing a range of jobs around the house. Don't panic! I'm not thinking about a particularly large range! In fact, I'm thinking of a very small range: probably jobs that you

1: Which is the same world that you live in, only a bit taller.

would do anyway, like cleaning your shoes, tidying your room — no, hang on, I think they're probably bad examples! Look, I'll leave you to figure out exactly which jobs you feel fall into this category. After all, you know your parents better than I do, so you probably have a better idea of what you can get away with. Now you may be thinking: "Hold on a minute! Why bother with wages? Why not just get an increase in allowance?" So let's get that out of the way right now. Let us suppose that your allowance is fifteen dollars (we can all dream!) and you negotiate wages of an extra five dollars for walking the dog, cleaning up the yard after the dog and doing the dishes three times a week.

That sounds about right to me. But why don't we just call it twenty dollars allowance and be done with it? Simple; because when you want to negotiate an allowance increase, your parents will base it on twenty dollars, which is quite a decent amount of allowance, as opposed to fifteen dollars, which sounds like a lot less. Also, the advantage of receiving two separate amounts is that you have two amounts to negotiate (i.e. increase) instead of just one. One bit of advice: make sure that you negotiate your allowance and your wages separately. I suggest you try for more allowance about a month after each birthday. Your argument should be that now that you're a year older, you need more money. On the wages front, listen out for any talk about your mum or dad getting a pay raise themselves; this would definitely be a good time to move in and start talking about inflation, and the way that the going rate for dog-walking has gone up. The dog is also older and therefore harder to walk.

If you approach all these negotiations with a reasonable amount of caution, you should be able to increase your income month by month. Add to this any one-off payments you get for washing the car or mowing the lawn, and you could soon be earning more than your parents!

"X" amount

What is it?
This is the sort of thing people say when they don't want you to know exactly how much they're talking about. Parents use it so that you won't be able to figure out how much they earn.

Example: "Soandso said that if I give him 'X amount' he'll let me have the whatyacallit." Talking in code, or what? Let's face it, that could mean anything. It could mean:

"Johnnie Elastic said that if I give him forty thousand dollars in unmarked bills he'll let me have the Porsche." Or it could mean:

"Mr. Willikers said that if I give him a dollar he'll let me have the bag of homemade gumdrops his wife made."

You can never tell, but it's safe to assume that if parents talk in code, they've got something to hide. Either that or they've been watching too many James Bond movies.

You see, their biggest fear is that if you find out how much they earn, you'll be pushing them for much more allowance, wages, birthday money, etc. Likewise, they'd never get you to wash the car again, because you'd turn around and say: "Hey! The amount you earn you could buy a new one every time the car got dirty!"

How to cope

There's really nothing to cope with. But it is worth mentioning that if your parents use the term "X amount," they are far more likely to be disguising a *large* amount than a *small* one. If they use the term a lot, this could be a good time to move in and try to negotiate a "pay" raise.

A word of warning. It's possible that if you push your negotiations too much, your parents will say something along the lines of: "You don't pay *us* for being your parents."

This is the kind of ludicrous logic that only a parent is capable of, and is quickly dismissed by saying: "No, but I never wanted you as my parents. I wanted Mr. and Mrs. Wang, up the road, who have seven cars and their own swimming pool." That'll shut them up!

Your own wheels

What are they?
In your case, we're probably talking about a bike, although, no doubt, you're already dreaming of the day when you can have your own car. But for now, you're going to have to make do with a bike. There are two distinct types of bike: the one you save up for and buy yourself, otherwise known as the Dream Machine, and the one your parents buy you, otherwise known as the Complete Waste of Space.

Why is it that anything your parents buy you is almost certainly going to cause the Fashion Police to turn up on your doorstep, batter your door in with metal bars and cart you off to be tortured and interrogated within an inch of your life? When will parents realize that garbage often costs the same as decent stuff?[1] Never, frankly. When it comes to bikes, parents are very fond of saying things like: "What do you need twenty gears for?" What does your mum need thirty pairs of shoes for? After all, she's only got one pair of feet.[2]

This demonstrates a total lack of understanding of the way a modern bike works. The more gears you've got, the more energy you save when you're cycling. And saving energy is what life in the twenty-first century is all about. This is not an exercise bike we're talking about here; it's an efficient form of transport. Unfortunately,

1: Unless the garbage has designer wheels.
2: As far as you know.

your parents' childhood memory of a bike is something *their* parents bought them. It had three gears and a chain that kept coming off. With some of the bikes I've seen recently, it's hard to figure out where the chain *is*, let alone how it comes off.

So the obvious choice is buying your own "wheels": fast, efficient and with low maintenance. The only problem is *how*.

How to cope

Parents respond well to the idea that their children are saving up for something. It almost doesn't matter what. Although if they got wind of the fact that you were saving up in order to be able to fill your dad's bathwater with piranhas, they might have something to say about it.

So you want a bike, a big flashy one with more gears than is feasible on a bike of that size, and all the latest stuff: exactly the kind of bike that your parents will never let you have in a thousand years. So throughout the saving-up period, you've got to work on getting them used to the idea. There are two things to emphasize:

The enormous range of safety features that your chosen bike has, whether it has them or not. And . . .

The massive effort that you are putting into the whole saving experience.

Both of these will impress your parents enormously, because they both demonstrate how *mature* you've become. This sort of thing impresses parents, mainly because maturity is something that they're not too good at themselves. If you play this exactly right, you may even get your parents chipping in the odd few dollars every now and again, just to speed the whole process up. A word of caution: Never, ever show them a picture of your chosen bike, unless you want the whole thing to derail. (Not just the derailleurs.)

130

Eventually, you'll have saved enough money to buy your dream machine. You head down to the store to pick it up. DO NOT accept a ride from either (or both) of your parents. You really DO NOT want them in the store with you while you're buying your bike; this is partly because they'd try to get you to buy a *sensible* (i.e. ugly) one, and partly because, if the storeowner sees your parents, he might assume that you're all escaped lunatics and refuse to serve you.

Having bought your bike, you take it home. Leave it outside and do one last bit of PR about the wonders of the bike, how having so many gears is really a safety feature, and so on. Show them the safety helmet, reflective armbands and lights that you've bought to go with your new bike. Then, and only then, let your parents see it. Make sure that while they're looking at it, you continue to jabber on about how wonderful it is. This will prevent them from having any kind of a conversation about what *they* think about the bike.

None of this will make your parents *like* the bike, but probably the worst thing they'll do is shake their heads and assume that your poor choice of wheels has something to do with hormonal imbalance,[1] which is something neither they nor you have any control over. Problem solved: you have the bike of your choice, and you've also demonstrated that you're capable of being careful with money at the same time.

A word of advice: if you are saving for a bike, make sure that you allow enough money for a decent helmet. Yes, I know some of them look a bit nerdy, but there are a few cool ones, and if they help save your life, what does it matter if you look a little silly? Reflective strips are also important, because you do want motorists to see you cycling along. But to me, the most important things are bright lights, especially if you think you might need to ride your bike at night (most people do). Yes, I know that a lot of cyclists rely on reflectors these days, but unless a car's headlight beam hits the reflector directly, they don't show up at all. And even when they do, they're pretty pathetic. Lights, on the other hand, not only help you be *seen*, but they also help you to *see* — two things that are essential when riding a bike at night. Sorry; as you know I don't normally preach at you, but I've seen too many people knocked off their bikes not to mention it. Thank you. Lecture over. Let's go back to being funny(ish!).

1: Hormonal imbalance can be used to excuse pretty well anything, as long as you don't overdo it.

Zee end bit

What is it?

Well, it's the end of the book. I had to cheat a bit in the A–Z section because I can't always think of things that match the letters of the alphabet. So what? It's my book and I'll do as I please!

I hope that all of the above stuff has helped you understand the many, many different sides to money; how to get it, how to hang on to it and what to do with it when you get it. Of course, there are millions of things that I haven't told you. I haven't mentioned, for instance, that Henry VIII added cheap metal to gold and silver coins in Tudor times, presumably to save money.

When his daughter Elizabeth I came to the throne she had the coins remade, putting the gold back in.

133

I haven't told you that French soldiers serving in Canada in 1685 were paid in playing cards, because their wages were often delayed in being shipped from France.

Nor have I mentioned the Klondike gold rush in the mid-nineteenth century; or the fact that after the First World War (1918), inflation ran so high in Germany that by 1923, money was almost worthless; workmen were being paid twice a day, and taking their pay home in huge wicker baskets. A loaf of bread cost hundreds of marks.

In Italy, in the 1970s, there weren't enough small coins to go around, so shopkeepers used to give bags of candy as change! In Vietnam, they've used lipstick as money, and during the Second World War, people sometimes used cigarettes.

I also haven't told you that they mark the edges of coins to keep people from forging them; this is called graining. Check out a quarter, you'll see what I mean.

Did I mention that coins were exchanged as love tokens in medieval times? I don't think I did. I could also have told you that audiences in Shakespeare's time used to throw coins at the actors. Occasionally they hit one — that soon shut him up!

Did you know that in Fiji they used to use whales' teeth for money? Well, you do now. In fact, there's lots, lots more to discover about money. A book like this can only scratch the surface. But one thing I can tell you is the *secret* of money. How to make tons and tons of it. Would you like to know that? Would you like to be so rich that you couldn't count your money, even if you stayed up all day and night and didn't even have time to watch TV? Well, here it is:

THE SECRET OF MONEY

Oh, no! I've run out of book! You'll just have to find out the secret for yourselves. And if you do . . . do you think you could let me know what it is, please?